PACIFIC COAST INSHORE FISHES

by

Daniel W. Gotshall

SEA CHALLENGERS ● LOS OSOS, CALIFORNIA

WESTERN MARINE ENTERPRISES ● VENTURA, CALIFORNIA

1981

A SEA CHALLENGERS AND
WESTERN MARINE ENTERPRISES PUBLICATION

©1981 Daniel W. Gotshall   Second Printing

FRONT COVER

Rosy rock fish, *Sebastes rosaseus*, by Daniel W. Gotshall.
Printed by Dai Nippon Printing Co., Ltd., Tokyo, Japan.

ISBN: 0-930030-31-1 (Paperbound)

Library of Congress Catalog Card Number: 80-53-27

Second, completely revised edition; formerly *Fishwatchers' Guide to the Inshores Fishes of the Pacific Coast.*

SEA CHALLENGERS
1851 Don Avenue
Los Osos, California 93402

WESTERN MARINE ENTERPRISES
Box Q
Ventura, California 93002

Phototypesetting and pre-press production by Padre Productions.

FOREWORD

I tried for a lot of years to get my wife, Arline, to go snorkeling with me, but to no avail. No amount of explaining what a beautiful new world would be revealed for her to explore could induce her to put on a face mask and paddle around at the surface. I pointed out that she wouldn't have to dive to enjoy this sport, but that didn't work either. Nor did cajoling or threatening. Then in 1979, while in Hawaii on a vacation, some friends were doing so much oohing and aahing over the fishes, corals, and other marine life that they could see through a face mask that Arline could hold off no longer. Once she found out what she had been missing, I had to purchase a face mask for her just to get mine back.

I still could not convince her that the underwater world off California was every bit as rich and colorful as that of the tropics until she saw the beautiful photographs that Dan Gotshall had taken and was including in *Pacific Coast Inshore Fishes*. Now I can say that I have absolute faith in the old adage that a single picture is worth a thousand words. In this case, an assortment of pictures accomplished what I had been unable to do during several decades of wordiness. I firmly believe that Arline now is convinced that there is more to do at the beach than swim or lie on the warm sand.

Occasionally, while perusing the text, I found myself thinking how interesting it would have been to have had Dan include brief mention, where apropos, of this or that behavioral trait, habitat choice or puzzling habit peculiar to a given species – in addition to those he does discuss, that is. However, by the time I had finished the text, I realized that Dan had interwoven just the right kind of text and pictures to make a truly first rate presentation. With the information given, the reader will have sufficient background for observing odds and ends of behavior, color, size, habitat preference, etc., and for discussing his observations authoritatively. Knowledge of the information contained between the covers of *Pacific Coast Inshore Fishes* certainly can save the interested fisherman, shore scrounger, snorkeler, diver, underwater photographer, or amateur ichthyologist a lot of the "learning time" that we, as professionals, had to extend in order to justify our existence.

John E. Fitch
September 1980

DEDICATION

This book is dedicated to my wife, Ann, for her continuing patience and support, and to all who share a sense of wonder for the abundance, diversity and variety of marine life along our unique Pacific Coast.

Daniel W. Gotshall

TABLE OF CONTENTS

INTRODUCTION

This field guide is a completely revised edition of *Fishwatchers' Guide to the Inshore Fishes of the Pacific Coast.* In this new edition I have strived to correct the deficiencies of the first edition by expanding the number of species described to 126, using new photographs, and completely redoing the color separations on all of the color plates. I have also attempted to include the latest information available on geographical and depth ranges and changes in scientific and common names. In this edition you will find not only a narrative key to the families but also a pictorial key. I have also added a section on common species to be found in the various types of habitats, i.e., sand, kelp beds, and rocky reefs, by geographical areas.

As was the first edition, this book is designed for the growing company of "fish-watchers"—people who, through their interest in fishing, snorkeling, SCUBA diving, natural history or ecology, have come into contact with the fascinating and somewhat bewildering world of the fishes, and have sought to learn more about them. The key to this knowledge is identification. Once you know an animal's name, everything else begins to fall into place. Unfortunately, one soon learns that, for most parts of the world, there is little in the way of compact and accurate guides designed for non-specialists. On the Pacific Coast of North America, the last major work on the subject addressed to amateurs was the beautiful *Marine Game Fish of the Pacific Coast from Alaska to the Equator* by Lionel Walford, published by the Santa Barbara Museum of Natural History in 1937. Only 1,500 copies of this work were ever printed and today it is a collector's item, commanding hundreds of dollars in the rare book market.

More than 600 species of fish have been reported off the Pacific Coast of North America. In setting the limits of this book, I have set out to describe and picture those species most commonly observed by snorkelers and SCUBA divers in waters ranging from about 10 to about 150 feet. I have eliminated the well known game fish, the small fish that live in the turbid region near the shore and that tend to be difficult to identify, and fish that are extremely rare. I have also limited myself to species that can be identified alive in the water. For each species, I provide: nomenclature, range, depth, habitat, size, and distinguishing characteristics (field marks), and, for all but five, there is a full color photograph of a living specimen in its natural habitat.

To the best of my knowledge, the information presented here is the best and most recent available, but, since only a tiny fraction of the members of any species are ever taken for scientific observation, the reader must make allowance for error. This is especially true for range and depth information; the limits given here are simply those believed to be reported reliably. Unless otherwise specified, sizes given are the maximums reported to date, and the average adult will be somewhat smaller. Some of the information reported here is new and has never been published previously. Such cases are indicated by an asterisk in the text (*).

NOMENCLATURE. For each species, I give the common name, the scientific name, and a translation of the scientific name. The common name is really the *most* common name—the name by which the species is known to scientists and usually non-scientists. These names are not standardized and are subject to some local variation. The scientific or Latin names are standardized. They are the same throughout the world; the first word is the name of the genus to which the fish belongs, and the second is its specific name. Generally, a species is comprised of freely inter-breeding individuals, and a genus is a group of closely related species. Underneath the scientific names, I have provided translations of the Latin words and, occasionally, brief explanations. The symbol (→) means that the translation is reversed; that is, the first term of the translation corresponds to the second term of the Latin.

HOW TO USE THIS BOOK. If you have the fish in hand, begin with the Key on Page 12. Using both these clues and the drawings on Page 16 you will be able to narrow your specimen down to one or two families. The key will direct you to the right part of the text. If you have observed the fish but not collected it, refer to the drawings on Page 16, then when you have decided on which family or families it might belong to, turn to the color plates to confirm your identification. Examine the photographs carefully, and refer to the text. The best guide is usually habitat; fish found in kelp beds are unlikely to be found far away from them. Behavior is another good clue and so is range if you interpret it broadly enough. A species reported as far south as Puget Sound is unlikely to appear off Point Conception. Field marks are usually reliable, but often you must get a good look, and you must know something about fish anatomy. The chart and glossary on Pages 9-11 will help you here.

NEW INFORMATION. As I have said, there is much that is not known about the fish of our region. In recent years, however, the increased popularity of salt water activities has been a real boon to the ichthyologist as a steady stream of new data and good leads have come in from interested amateurs. If you do come upon something that doesn't fit with the information in this book, I would very much like to know about it. Please address the author at: Sea Challengers, 1851 Don Ave., Los Osos, California 93402.

ACKNOWLEDGMENTS

This revised edition is the product of many individuals. To all of those listed below, and also to anyone I may have inadvertently overlooked, I owe a great debt of gratitude:

Robert N. Lea, California Department of Fish and Game, served as technical and general editor of the manuscript; he also provided up to date taxonomic, size and distribution information on several species; Lillian Dempster, Curator of Fishes, California Academy of Sciences, translated several of the scientific names; Daniel J. Miller, California Department of Fish and Game, provided all of the excellent drawings; John Fitch, California Department of Fish and Game, read the manuscript and provided information for several species; David Behrens, Biologist, Pacific Gas and Electric Co., reviewed the galleys; Jack Engle, Catalina Marine Science Center, University of Southern California and Andrew Lissnor, Interstate Electronics Co., provided new depth ranges for several species; Robert Lavenberg, Curator of Fishes, Los Angeles County Museum of Natural History, provided taxonomic data; the maps were drawn by Laurence L. Laurent; Phyllis Johnson typed the original manuscript, and assisted with the preparation of the Glossary.

PHOTO CREDITS

Photographer	Species Number
Lou Barr	20, 111
David Behrens	105
Tony Chess	7, 13
Gordon Cox	2
Casey Jones	114
Laurence Laurent	124
Ken Lucas	5, 69, 77, 120, 125
David McCray	6
Beth Mulcahy	113
Rick Rosenthal	18, 53, 54, 118
Charles Turner (deceased)	11, 74, 75, 115, 126

All other photographs by Daniel Gotshall.

ILLUSTRATED GLOSSARY

abdominal
In fish, assuming the pectoral fin is lying flat to the body, refers to the attachment of the pelagic fins between anus and middle of pectoral fins (See figure 1).

adipose fin
An additional small, fleshy fin found on the midline near the tail in certain fishes such as the lizardfish; consists mostly of fatty tissue.

anterior
Of, toward, on or near the front or head region of the fish's body.

barbel
Any of the slender, fleshy, whiskerlike growths on the chin or lips of certain fishes such as the Pacific tomcod.

canine teeth
Large, sharp, cone-shaped teeth used for grasping prey.

cirri (Plural of cirrus)
Fringelike skin flaps on top of head (for example see fringeheads pg. 76) or other parts of body.

coronal spines
The head spine on certain rockfishes (Scorpaenidae) located at the rear of the bony ridge between the eyes.

cryptic
Hidden, tending to conceal or camouflage as "cryptic coloring;" tends to hide in caves or holes.

dorsal
Of, toward, on, in or near the back of a fish, or pertaining to the upper surface of the back.

fin membrane
Thin connective tissue found between the spines and rays of the fins of a fish.

gill arch
The curved bone located inside the gill cavity of bony fishes which supports the fish's gills; contains bony toothlike structures on the forward edges called gill rakers.

gill rakers
The bony toothlike projections on the forward edges of gill arches (see above) that function to protect the gills and strain food.

hermaphroditic
Possessing both male and female sex organs in one fish; sometimes, possessing first one set of sex organs and then the opposite set of sex organs alternately in the same fish.

jugular
In fish, refers to the attachment of pelvic fins between rear edge of gill cover and rear edge of eye (see figure 1).

lateral line
A line of modified scales containing sensory pores that generally runs along the side of the fish from the back of the head to the tail fin.

mandible
In fish, the lower jaw; also the bone of the lower jaw.

maxillary
Pertains to the main bone of an animal's upper jaw. In some fish the maxillary, or jaw bone, may form the whole jaw, in others only the back portion of the jaw.

molar teeth
Broad, rounded teeth adapted for grinding and located toward the back of the mouth.

nape
Back of neck.

nocturnal
Describes fish that normally sleep during the day and become active at night.

ocellus	A pigmented, usually ringed, eyelike spot; any spot on a fish resembling an eye.
opercular spine	Bony spines located on the rear edge of the gill cover (see above).
operculum	The bony flap covering gills in higher fishes.
ovoviviparous	A type of reproduction in which fertilized eggs are retained, nurtured and hatched *inside* the female. The eggs receive some nutrients and oxygen from the female, but do not develop a real placenta attaching them to the mother's body as in mammalian reproduction.
papillae (Plural of papilla)	Any small, soft, rounded, nipplelike projections or protuberances anywhere on a fish.
photophores	Specialized, well-defined, light-producing organs found in certain fishes; usually with a lens and round reflector.
posterior	Of, toward, on, in or near the rear or tail region of the fish's body.
premaxillary	Refers to either of two bones located in front of maxillary bones (see above).
preopercular spine	Any spines located on the rear edge of the preopercular bone (see figure 1).
soft rays	The segmented and often branched soft bony spines that support the membrance of the fins of a fish.
spine	A sharp, projecting fin ray that is neither segmented nor branched; usually rigid and helps support the membrane of the fins of a fish. Sometimes flexible, at other times sharp, rigid and capable of causing injury.
suborbital stay	A usually thin membrane-type bone located below the orbit of the eye and under the skin (see figure 1).
symphyseal knob	The bony knob located beneath the tip of the lower jaw (see figure 1), particularly on rockfish (Scorpaenidae).
thoracic	In fish, refers to the attachment of pelvic fins between middle of pectoral fins and the rear edge of the maxillary (see figure 1).
ventral	Of, toward, on, in or near the abdominal area, or pertaining to the lower or under surface of a fish.
viviparous	Method of reproduction utilized by nearly all mammals in which living young (rather than eggs) are maintained inside the mother's body and nourished via a placenta until ready for birth.

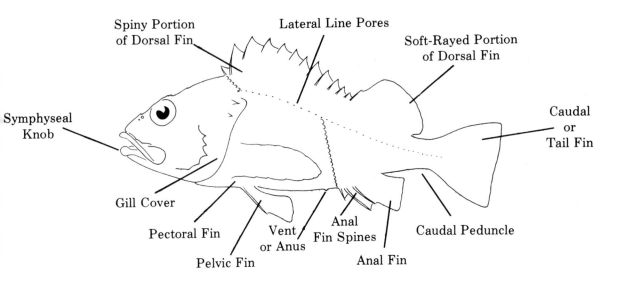

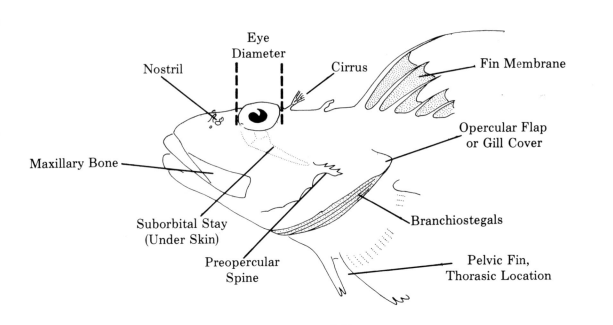

FIGURE 1

Parts of a Bony Fish

(Drawings by Daniel J. Miller)

11

FAMILY KEY

A key is simply a series of choices. Each choice leads you either to another numbered choice or to the Family you are looking for. For example, Choice 1 leads you to either Choice 12 or Choice 2; Choice 2 leads to either Choice 3 or Choice 8; Choice 3 leads either to Choice 4 or Choice 5; and so on.

28A Anal fin without spines. Family Cottidae (Sculpins) ....(p. 52)
  B Anal fin with spines 29

29A Ridges and spines on head; 4 to 11 soft anal rays. Family Scorpaenidae
  (Scorpionfishes)...(p. 34)
  B No ridges or spines on head; 12 or more soft anal rays. Family
  Hexagrammidae (Greenlings) ....(p. 48)

30A Lateral line terminates below posterior portion of dorsal fin. Family
  Pomacentridae (Damselfishes)...............................(p. 70)
  B Lateral line extends at least to base of caudal fin....................31

31A One or two anal spines 32
  B Three or four anal spines 33

32A Single dorsal fin. Family **Malacanthidae** (Tilefishes)..............(p. 60)
  B Two dorsal fins, in some cases connected by membrane. Family
  Sciaenidae (Drums)..(p. 62)

33A Two anal spines isolated from fin. Family Carangidae (Jacks) .....(p. 60)
  B Anal spines connected to soft rays...............................34

34A Maxillary does not reach eye; snout pointed. Family Chaetodontidae
  (Butterflyfishes) ....(p. 66)
  B Not as above 35

35A Sheath of scales extends out onto dorsal fin. Family Embiotocidae
  (Surfperches) ....**(p. 64)**
  B No sheath of scales on dorsal fin...............................36

36A Maxillary mostly hidden by sliding under bone above when mouth
  closed 37
  B Maxillary fully exposed when mouth closed; three spines on opercle.
  Family Serranidae (Sea basses)..............................(p. 58)

37A Anterior teeth minute and numerous, not canine-like or incisor-like;
  Anal rays: 10 or 11; lateral line extends out onto caudal rays. Family
  Haemulidae (Grunts) ....(p. 60)
  B Anterior teeth either canine-like or incisor-like; lateral line does not
  extend out onto caudal rays; anal rays 12 or more 38

38A Anterior teeth canine-like. Family Labridae (Wrasses) ....(p. 72)
  B Anterior teeth incisor-like or conical. Family Kyphosidae
  (Sea chubs)...(p. 62)

39A Anal and dorsal fins continuous with caudal fin. Family Ophidiidae
  (Cusk-eels) ....(p. 32)
  B Anal and dorsal fins separate from caudal fin 40

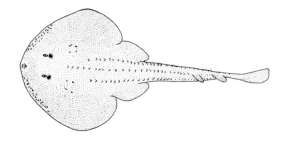

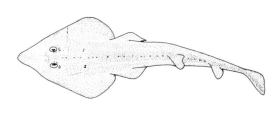

1. THORNBACKS, 1. RHINOBATIDAE   P. 26   2. GUITARFISHES, RHINOBATIDAE   P. 28

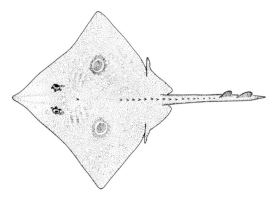

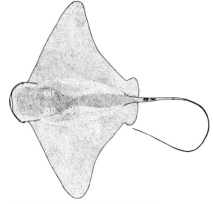

3. SKATES, RAJIDAE   P. 28   4. EAGLE RAYS, MYLIOBATIDAE   P. 28

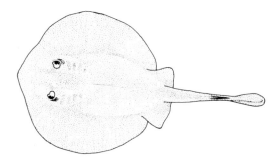

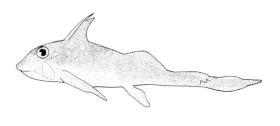

5. STINGRAYS, DASYATIDAE   P. 28   6. RATFISHES, CHIMAERIDAE   P.30

FIGURE 2 Pictorial Key to the Fish Families
(Drawings by Daniel J. Miller, from Miller and Lea, 1976)

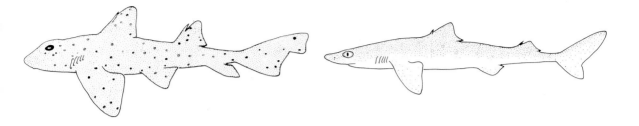

7. HORNSHARKS, HETERODONTIDAE   P. 24   8. DOGFISHES, SQUALIDAE   P. 24

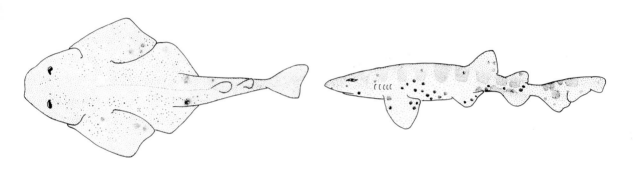

9. ANGEL SHARKS, SQUATINIDAE   P. 24   10. CAT SHARKS, SCYLIORHINIDAE   P. 24

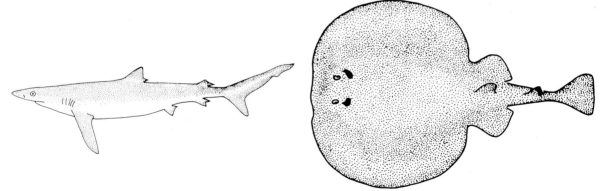

11. REQUIEM SHARKS, CARCHARHINIDAE   P. 26   12. ELECTRIC RAYS, TORPEDINIDAE   P. 26

FIGURE 2 Pictorial Key to the Fish Families
(Drawings by Daniel J. Miller, from Miller and Lea, 1976)

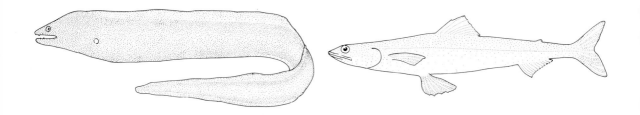

13. MORAYS, MURAENIDAE   P. 30   **14. LIZARD FISHES, SYNODONTIDAE**   P. 30

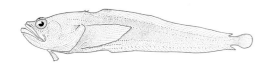

15. TOADFISHES, BATRACHOIDIDAE   P. 30   **16. CUSK-EELS, OPHIDIIDAE**   P. 32

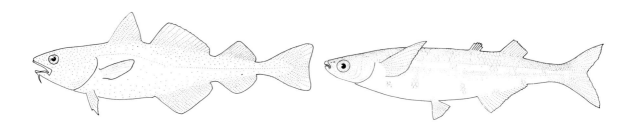

17. CODFISHES, GADIDAE   P. 32   **18. SILVERSIDES, ATHERINIDAE**   P. 34

FIGURE 2 Pictorial Key to the Fish Families
(Drawings by Daniel J. Miller, from Miller and Lea, 1976)

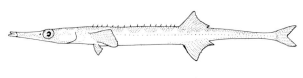 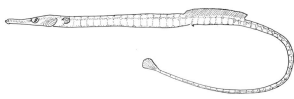

19. TUBESNOUTS, GASTEROSTEIDAE   P. 34   20. PIPEFISHES, SYNGNATHIDAE   P. 34

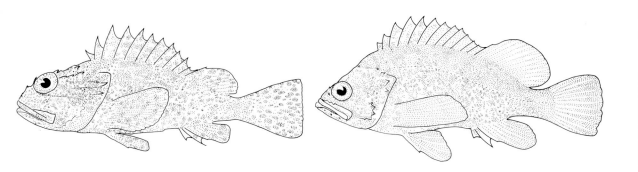

21. SCORPIONFISHES, SCORPAENIDAE   P. 34

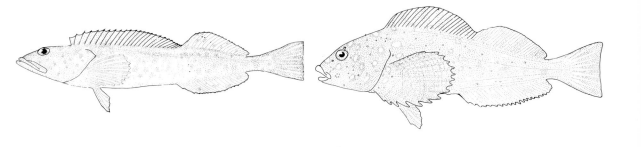

22. GREENLINGS, HEXAGRAMMIDAE   P. 48

FIGURE 2 Pictorial Key to the Fish Families
(Drawings by Daniel J. Miller, from Miller and Lea, 1976)

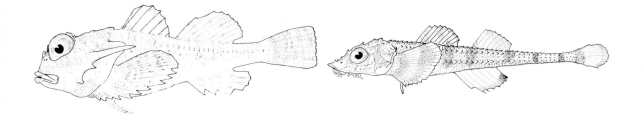

23. SCULPINS, COTTIDAE   P. 52   24. POACHERS, AGONIDAE   P. 56

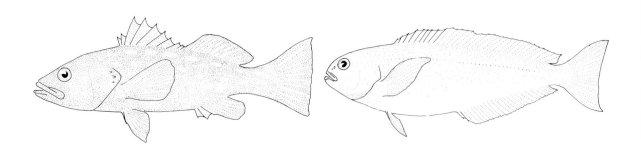

25. SEA BASSES, SERRANIDAE   P. 58   26. TILE FISHES, **MALACANTHIDAE**   P. 60

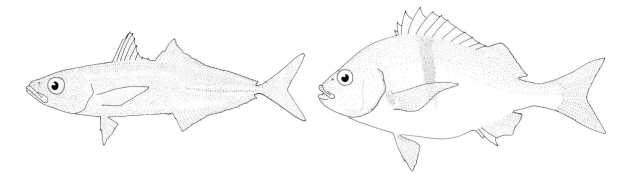

27. JACKS, CARANGIDAE   P. 62   28. GRUNTS, **HAEMULIDAE**   P. 62

FIGURE 2 Pictorial Key to the Fish Families
(Drawings by Daniel J. Miller, from Miller and Lea, 1976)

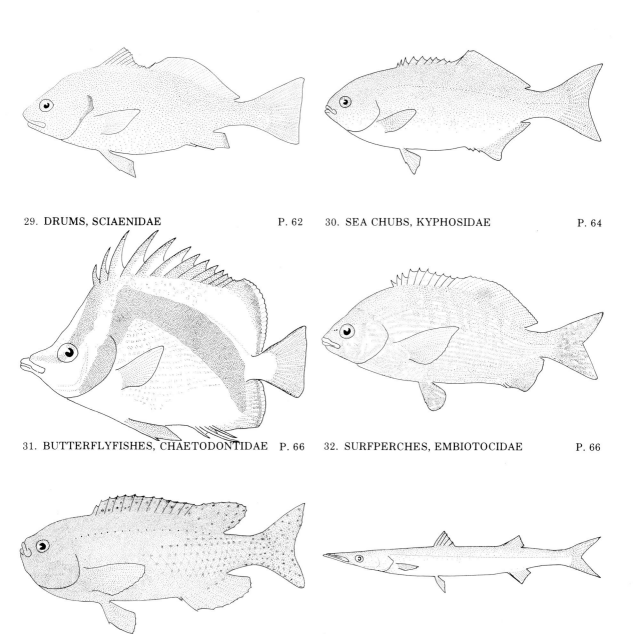

29. DRUMS, SCIAENIDAE   P. 62   30. SEA CHUBS, KYPHOSIDAE   P. 64

31. BUTTERFLYFISHES, CHAETODONTIDAE   P. 66   32. SURFPERCHES, EMBIOTOCIDAE   P. 66

33. DAMSELFISHES, POMACENTRIDAE   P. 70   34. BARRACUDAS, SPHYRAENIDAE   P. 70

FIGURE 2 Pictorial Key to the Fish Families
(Drawings by Daniel J. Miller, from Miller and Lea, 1976)

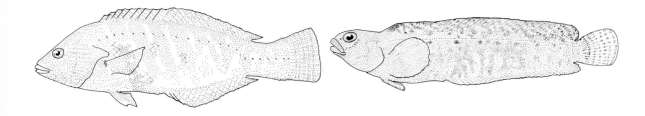

35. WRASSES, LABRIDAE   P. 70   36. RONQUILS, BATHYMASTERIDAE   P. 74

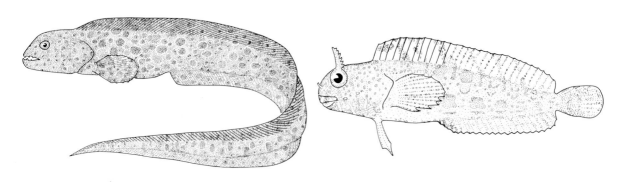

37. WOLFFISHES, ANARHICHADIDAE   P. 74   38. COMBTOOTH BLENNIES, BLENNIIDAE   P. 76

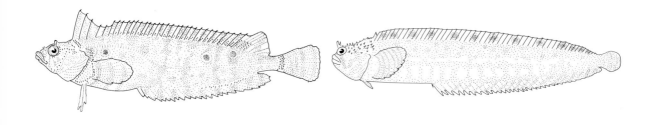

39. CLINIDS, CLINIDAE   P. 76   40. PRICKELBACKS, STICHAEIDAE   P. 78

FIGURE 2 Pictorial Key to the Fish Families
(Drawings by Daniel J. Miller, from Miller and Lea, 1976)

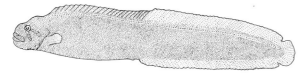 

40. PRICKELBACKS, STICHAEIDAE   P. 78   41. GOBIES, GOBIIDAE   P. 80

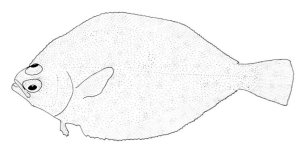 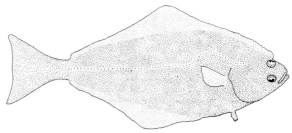

42. LEFTEYED FLOUNDERS, BOTHIDAE   P. 80   43. RIGHTEYED FLOUNDERS,
PLEURONECTIDAE   P. 82

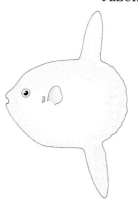

44. MOLAS, MOLIDAE   P. 86

FIGURE 2 Pictorial Key to the Fish Families
(Drawings by Daniel J. Miller, from Miller and Lea, 1976)

FAMILY HETERODONTIDAE

1.   HORN SHARK   *Heterodontus francisci*

(San Franciscan ←→ mixed-tooth)

Identification: A brown or grey colored shark with large black spots on body, and spines in front of each dorsal fin.

Natural History: This nocturnal shark usually rests on bottom during daylight. Horn sharks lay eggs; each is surrounded by a distinctive, grenade shaped, horny case.

Size: Length to 48 inches (122 cm).

Range and Habitat: Monterey, California to the Gulf of California, but not recorded from southern part of gulf. Common around shallow rocky reefs in southern California. Maximum reported depth is 500 feet (153 m).

FAMILY SQUALIDAE

2.   SPINY DOGFISH   *Squalus acanthias*

(Spine; shark)

Identification: This common shark also has spines in front on each dorsal fin, but it lacks the bull-shaped head and black spots of the horn shark.

Natural History: The developing 2 to 20 embryos receive no nourishment from the female (Ovoviviparous).

Size: Length to 5 feet, 2 inches (157 cm).

Range and Habitat: Temperate and subtropical Atlantic and Pacific Oceans; on our coast from Alaska to central Baja California over sand and mud bottoms. Occasionally seen near reefs in British Columbia. The maximum recorded depth is 2,400 feet (732 m).

FAMILY SQUATINIDAE

3.   PACIFIC ANGEL SHARK   *Squatina californica*

(California; skate)

Identification: The skate-like body is usually covered with brown spots; the gill slits are located in a notch on sides behind head. The mouth is located under the head as in skates, and many sharks.

Natural History: This common shark is also ovoviviparous.

Size: Length to 5 feet (152 cm), weight to 60 lbs. (27 kg).

Range and Habitat: Southeastern Alaska to the Gulf of California, but not recorded from British Columbia. Common around southern California Channel Islands, on sand and mud bottoms in shallow water.

FAMILY SCYLIORHINIDAE

4.   SWELL SHARK   *Cephaloscyllium ventriosum*

(pot-bellied; head shark)

Identification: The only spotted and mottled shallow water shark in our area with the first dorsal fin located behind origin of pelvic fins.

Natural History: This cryptic, sedentary shark lays individual eggs in distinctive amber colored cases.

Size: Length to 3.3 feet (102 cm).

Range and Habitat: Monterey Bay, California to the Gulf of California; around shallow reefs in caves and crevices; in depths from shallow water to 1,380 feet (421 m).

1. HORN SHARK

2. SPINY DOGFISH

3. PACIFIC ANGEL SHARK

4. SWELL SHARK

FAMILY CARCHARHINIDAE

5. **LEOPARD SHARK**   *Triakis semifasiata*
(Three point; half-banded)
Identification: The large black bars and spots on the body separate this shark from
all other requiem sharks.
Size: Length to 6.5 feet (198 cm).
Range and Habitat: Oregon to the Gulf of California; on sand and mud bottoms in
bays and shallow inshore waters.

6. **BLUE SHARK**   *Prionace glauca*
(Blue ↔ Saw-point)
Identification: This common surface (Epipelagic) shark can be readily identified by
the striking blue color above and grey-white below and the long sabre-like pectoral fin.
Natural History: Up to 60 young sharks develop within the female. The adults feed
on salmon, lanternfishes, squid and other small fish.
Size: Length to 13 feet (390 cm).
Range and Habitat: Worldwide, in eastern Pacific from the Gulf of Alaska to Chile.
Common in our coastal surface water during late summer.

FAMILY TORPEDINIDAE

7. **PACIFIC ELECTRIC RAY**   *Torpedo californica*
(California ↔ electric ray)
Identification: The only ray in our area that lacks spines or prickles. The large caudal
fin and spots on the dorsal surface are also distinctive.
Natural History: These rays lack a venomous spine but are capable of producing a
strong electrical shock of up to 80 volts. They are aggressive and divers have reported
unprovoked attacks. Young develop within female.
Size: Length to 4 feet (122 cm), weight to 90 lbs. (41 kg).
Range and Habitat: Queen Charlotte Islands, British Columbia to Sebastian Viscaino
Bay, Baja California; on mud and sand bottoms; to depths of 1,380 feet (421 m).

FAMILY RHINOBATIDAE

8. **THORNBACK**   *Platyrhinoidis triseriata*
(Broad snout; three rows)
Identification: The three rows of prominant spines on the dorsal surface of adults and
the two dorsal fins are good identification characters.
Size: Length to 2.5 feet (76 cm), weight to 5.8 lbs. (2.6 kg).
Range and Habitat: San Francisco, California to Thurloe Head, Baja California; on
sand and mud bottoms; to depths of 150 feet (46 m).

5. LEOPARD SHARK

6. BLUE SHARK

7. PACIFIC ELECTRIC RAY

8. THORN BACK

9.   **BANDED GUITARFISH**   *Zapteryx exasperata*
                                               (Thin; made rough)
Identification: Two guitarfishes occur in our area: the banded guitarfish differs from
the shovelnose guitarfish (*Rhinobatus productus*, not illustrated) by having a disc
about as wide as long in adults and many darks bands across the back.
Size: *Zapteryx exasperata*: Length to 36 inches (91 cm); *Rhinobatus productus*:
Length to: 61.5 inches (156 cm).
Range and Habitat: *Zapteryx exasperata*: Newport Beach, California to Panama;
Rhinobatus productus: San Francisco, California, to the Gulf of California. Both occur
on sand bottoms in shallow water.

FAMILY RAJIDAE
10.   **BIG SKATE**   *Raja binoculata*
                                               (Two eyed ⟷ skate)
Identification: The big skate is the only member of the family, which contains about
8 species, in our area, commonly encountered by divers and can be distinguished by
the two large eye spots (ocelli), one on each wing, and the pelvic fins with a shallow
notch.
Natural History: Skates lay their eggs in individual horny cases.
Size: Length to 96 inches (244 cm).
Range and Habitat: Bering Sea to Cedros Island, Baja California; on sand and mud
bottoms; in depths from 10 to 360 feet (3 to 110 m).

FAMILY MYLIOBATIDAE
11.   **BAT RAY**   *Myliobatis californica*
                                               (California ⟷ grinder ray)
Identification: The only stingray in our area with a large head that protrudes beyond
the anterior edge of its pectoral fins.
Natural History: The name "grinder" comes from the flat grinding teeth bat rays use
to crush clams and oysters.
Size: Width to 57 inches (122 cm), weight to 210 lbs. (95 kg).
Range and Habitat: Oregon to the Gulf of California; in bays and other shallow sandy
or mud bottoms; out to depths of 100 feet (30 m).

FAMILY DASYATIDAE
12.   **ROUND STINGRAY**   *Urolophus halleri*
               (Tail-crest; after Mr. Haller, who was stung by this ray)
Identification: The almost circular disc, sometimes mottled or with spots or other
markings, is distinctive.
Natural History: Feed on shrimps, crabs, snails and clams.
Size: Length to 22 inches (56 cm).
Range and Habitat: Humboldt Bay, California to Panama; on sand and mud bottoms,
occasionally on reefs; in depths to 70 feet (21 m).

9. BANDED GUITARFISH

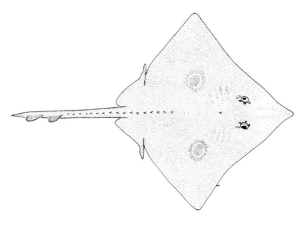

10. BIG SKATE

C. Turner

11. BAT RAY

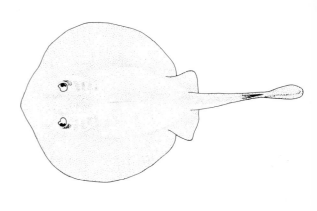

12. ROUND STINGRAY

FAMILY CHIMAERIDAE

13. **RATFISH**   **Hydrolagus colliei**

(Collie's, after M. Collie, naturalist ←→ water hare)

Identification: This close relative to sharks and rays can easily be recognized by its smooth skin, long tapering tail and bulky snout.

Natural History: Eggs are laid in elongated, ridged, brown cases.

Size: Length to 38 inches (96 cm).

Range and Habitat: Southeastern Alaska to Sebastian Viscaino Bay, Baja California, and an isolated population in upper Gulf of California; on soft bottoms; from shallow depths to 1,200 feet (366 m).

FAMILY MURAENIDAE

14. **CALIFORNIA MORAY**   *Gymnothorax mordax*

(Biting ←→ naked breast)

Identification: This is the only member of the family in our area and can be distinguished from other eel-like fishes by the lack of pectoral and pelvic fins.

Natural History: Morays feed on crabs, fish, lobster and sea urchins.

Size: Length to 5 feet (152 cm).

Range and Habitat: Point Conception, California to Magdalena Bay, Baja California; in rocky caves and crevices; from shallow water to about 130 feet (40 m).

FAMILY SYNODONTIDAE

15. **CALIFORNIA LIZARDFISH**   *Synodus lucioceps*

(Pike-head ←→ fish)

Identification: The body shape, broad head, and adipose fin instead of a rayed second dorsal are good distinguishing characters.

Natural History: Lizardfish feed on other fish and squid.

Size: Length to 25.2 inches (64 cm).

Range and Habitat: San Francisco, California to Guaymas, Mexico on sand and mud bottoms; from 5 to 750 feet deep (2 to 229 m).

FAMILY BATRACHOIDIDAE

16. **PLAINFIN MIDSHIPMAN**   *Porichthys notatus*

(Spotted ←→ porefish)

Identification: The large head, scaleless body and luminous organs (photophores) are very distinctive. The plainfin midshipman can be separated from the specklefin midshipman, *P. myriaster* (not illustrated), by the lack of spots in any of its fins.

Size: Length to 15 inches (38 cm). *P. myriaster*, length to 20 inches (51 cm).

Range and Habitat: *P. notatus*, Sitka, Alaska to the Gulf of California; *P. myriaster*, Pt. Conception, California to Magdalena Bay, Baja California; on sand and mud bottoms; out to depths of 1,000 feet (305 m) and 414 feet (126 m), respectively.

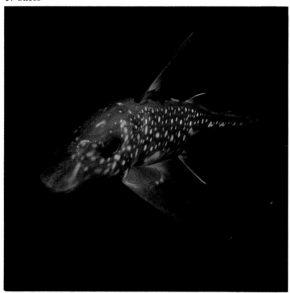

13. RATFISH

14. CALIFORNIA MORAY

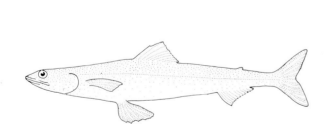

15. CALIFORNIA LIZARDFISH

16. PLAINFIN MIDSHIPMAN

31

FAMILY OPHIDIIDAE

17. **SPOTTED CUSK-EEL**   *Chilara taylori*
                                                    (Taylor's ←→ cusk-eel)

Identification: Distinguished by the eel-like body and pelvic fins near tip of lower jaw.
The spotted cusk-eel differs from the more southern basketweave cusk-eel, *Ophidion
scrippsae*(not illustrated) by having dark spotting on the back and sides.
Natural History: Cusk-eels burrow tail first into the sand or mud.
Size: Length to 14.3 inches (36 cm); *Ophidion scrippsae* to 10.8 inches (27 cm).
Range and Habitat: C. taylori, Oregon to Magdalena Bay*, Baja California; O. scrippsae,
Pt. Arguello to Magdalena Bay*, Baja California; on sand and mud bottoms; to depths
of 800 and 230 feet (244 and 70 m), respectively.

FAMILY GADIDAE

18. **PACIFIC TOMCOD**   *Microgadus proximus*
            (Small codfish; near -ref. to its close affinity to the Atlantic species)
Identification: Can be distinguished from other near shore cod in our area by the
lower jaw that is shorter than the upper, and a chin whisker (barbel) shorter than eye
diameter.
Size: Length to 12 inches (30 cm).
Range and Habitat: Unalaska Island, Alaska to Point Sal, California. A midwater and
bottom dweller; to depths of 1,200 feet (366 m).

19. **PACIFIC COD**   *Gadus macrocephalus*
                                                  (Large head ←→ Codfish)
Identification: The Pacific cod has a barbel as long as or longer than the diameter of
the eye.
Size: Length to 45 inches (114 cm).
Range and Habitat: Bering Sea to Santa Monica, California; over deep reefs and soft
bottoms; from 40 to 1,200 feet (12 to 366 m).

20. **WALLEYE POLLOCK**   *Theragra chalcogramma*
                                                  (Brass mark ←→ beast food)
Identification: Distinguished from other cods by the slightly projecting lower jaw
and the lack of a barbel.
Natural History: Walleye pollock feed on shrimp, herring, young salmon and other
fish. They in turn are fed on by seals.
Size: Length to 3 feet (91 cm).
Range and Habitat: Japan and Bering Sea, to off Carmel, California; over reefs and
soft bottoms; in depths near the surface to 690 feet (210 m).

R. Rosenthal

17. SPOTTED CUSK-EEL

18. PACIFIC TOMCOD

L. Barr

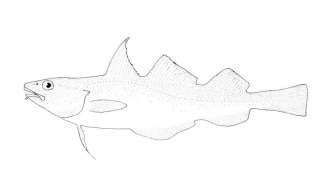

19. PACIFIC COD

20. WALLEYE POLLOCK

FAMILY ATHERINIDAE

21.   TOPSMELT   *Atherinops affinis*

(Like Atherina, a related genus; related)

Identification: Topsmelt can be distinguished from the larger jacksmelt, *Atherinopsis californiensis*(not illustrated), by the presence of 5 to 8 scales on the back between the two dorsal fins, and the forked teeth in one row. Jacksmelt have 10 to 12 scales between the dorsal fins, and no forked teeth.

Size: Length to 14.4 inches (36 cm); *Atherinopsis californiensis* to 17.5 inches (44 cm).

Range and Habitat: *Atherinops affinis*, Sooke Harbor, Vancouver Island, British Columbia to the Gulf of California; *Atherinopsis californiensis*, Yaquina, Oregon to Santa Maria Bay, Baja California; in bays, sloughs and other shallow waters.

FAMILY GASTEROSTEIDAE

22.   TUBESNOUT   *Aulorhynchus flavidus*

(Yellow ←→tube snout)

Identification: The long snout and 23 to 26 isolated spines in front of the dorsal fin are distinctive.

Natural History: Tubesnouts are nest builders; the nests are constructed and defended by the males.

Size: Length to 7 inches (18 cm).

Range and Habitat: Prince William Sound, Alaska to Point Rompiente, Baja California; in eel grass and kelp beds; from shallow bays to 100 feet (30 m).

FAMILY SYNGNATHIDAE

23.   BAY PIPEFISH   *Syngnathus leptorhynchus*

(Slender snout ←→ together jaws)

Identification: The bay pipefish differs from the other pipefish in our area by having 17 to 22 body rings, 36 to 46 tail rings and 28 to 44 soft dorsal rays.

Natural History: Pipefish males are responsible for raising the eggs until they hatch; this is done within a specialized pouch.

Size: Length to 13.7 inches (34.8 cm*).

Range and Habitat: Sitka, Alaska to Black Warrior Lagoon, Baja California; in eel grass beds in bays.

FAMILY SCORPAENIDAE

24.   SPOTTED SCORPIONFISH   *Scorpaena guttata*

(Speckled ←→ dorsal spines)

Identification: Distinguished from other members of the family, that occur in shallow water in our area, by having only 8 to 10 dorsal soft rays.

Natural History: Spotted scorpionfish lay eggs embedded in transparent, pear shaped cases.

Size: Length to 17 inches (43 cm).

Range and Habitat: Santa Cruz, California to Uncle Sam Bank, Baja California and isolated population in the Gulf of California; on rocky reefs to 600 feet (183 m).

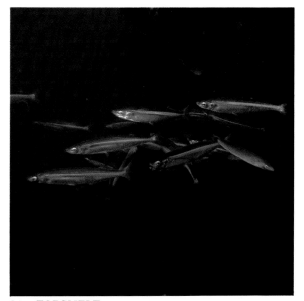

21. TOPSMELT

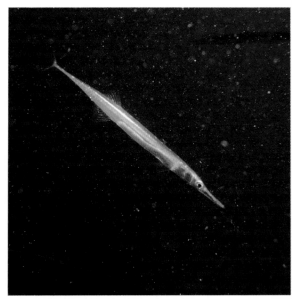

22. TUBESNOUT

23. BAY PIPEFISH

24. SPOTTED SCORPIONFISH

25. BOCACCIO

Sebastes paucispinis
(Magnificent; few spines)

Identification: The large mouth, with the maxillary extending to behind the eye, the dark back of the adult and spots on the juvenile will help separate the bocaccio from its look-alike, the **chilipepper**, *S. goodei* (**not illustrated**).

Natural History: As with all rockfish, the embryos develop into larvae within the female. Bocaccio feed mostly on other fishes.

Size: Length to 36 inches (91 cm).

Range and Habitat: Kodiak Island, Alaska to Punta Blanca, Baja California; over rocky reefs and soft bottoms; from the surface to 1,050 feet (320 m).

26. BLACK ROCKFISH

Sebastes melanops
(Magnificent; blackface)

Identification: Can be distinguished from the blue rockfish (27) and the dusky rockfish (28) by the larger maxillary that extends to beneath the rear of the eye and the rounded rear edge of the anal fin.

Natural History: Black rockfish feed on a variety of fishes, molluscs and crustaceans.

Size: Length to 23.8 inches (60 cm).

Range and Habitat: Amchitka Island, Alaska to Huntington Beach*, California; usually in large aggregations around rocky reefs and over soft bottoms; from the surface to 1200 feet (367 m).

27. BLUE ROCKFISH

Sebastes mystinus
(Magnificent; priest)

Identification: The blue rockfish can be separated from the dusky rockfish (28) by the lighter gray-blue mottling on the sides and the weak or absent symphyseal knob.

Natural History: Blue rockfish feed on a variety of the larger planktonic animals, including jellyfish and salps.

Size: Length to 21 inches (53 cm).

Range and Habitat: Bering Sea to Punta Banda, Baja California; around shallow rocky reefs; from surface to 300 feet (92 m).

28. DUSKY ROCKFISH

Sebastes ciliatus
(Magnificent; eyelashes)

Identification: The moderate symphyseal knob and greenish-brown body usually will separate the dusky rockfish from the blue rockfish (27).

Natural History: In Alaska the dusky and black rockfish are usually found near the same rock piles. Their food consists primarily of zooplankton.

Size: Length to 16 inches (41 cm).

Range and Habitat: Bering Sea and Gulf of Alaska to Dixon Entrance, British Columbia; around rocky reefs; in depths to 895 feet (273 m).

26. BLACK ROCKFISH

25. BOCACCIO **b) adult**

27. BLUE ROCKFISH **28. DUSKY ROCKFISH**

29. SQUARESPOT ROCKFISH   *Sebastes hopkinsi*

(Magnificent; after T. Hopkins, Esq.)

Identification: The long 2nd anal fin spine which extends beyond the tip of the 3rd spine and the dark blotches on and above the lateral line will separate the squarespot rockfish from the widow (30), yellowtail (31) and olive rockfishes (32).

Size: Length to 11.2 inches (29 cm).

Range and Habitat: Farallon Islands, California to Guadalupe Island, Baja California; around deep reefs; from 60 to 600 feet (18 to 183 m).

30. WIDOW ROCKFISH   *Sebastes entomelas*

(Magnificent; within black)

Identification: Widow rockfish have black membranes between the rays in the anal, pectoral, and pelvic fins. Their maxillary does not reach beyond the middle of the eye.

Natural History: Widow rockfish occur in very large aggregations in midwater where they feed on plankton.

Size: Length to 21 inches (53 cm).

Range and Habitat: Kodiak Island, Alaska to Todos Santos Bay, Baja California; around offshore reefs and in midwater; in depths to 1,200 feet (366 m).

31. YELLOWTAIL ROCKFISH   *Sebastes flavidus*

(Magnificent; yellow)

Identification: The yellowtail rockfish can usually be separated from its look-alike, the olive rockfish (32), by the two yellow areas on the gill cover, light orange-brown speckles on body scales and 8 soft-rays in the anal fin.

Natural History: Yellowtail rockfish have a homing instinct and will return to the reef where they were originally caught if given the opportunity.

Size: Length to 26 inches (66 cm).

Range and Habitat: Kodiak Island, Alaska to San Diego, California; around offshore reefs; to depths of 1800 feet (549 m).

32. OLIVE ROCKFISH   *Sebastes serranoides*

(Magnificent; resembling the sea-bass family)

Identification: Olive rockfish usually have 9 soft rays in the anal fin and lack the orange-brown speckles on the body scales of the yellowtail rockfish (31).

Natural History: Food consists mainly of fishes and squid.

Size: Length to 24 inches (61 cm).

Range and Habitat: Redding Rock, Humboldt County, California to San Benito Islands, Baja California; around reefs and in kelp beds; to depths of 480 feet (146 m).

29. SQUARESPOT ROCKFISH

30. WIDOW ROCKFISH

31. YELLOWTAIL ROCKFISH

32. OLIVE ROCKFISH

33. **PUGET SOUND ROCKFISH**   *Sebastes emphaeus*
                                                      (Magnificent; display)
Identification: Underwater the faded colors of the copper-red body with greenish-brown bars and blotches is distinctive.
Natural History: Females are mature at about 6 inches (15 cm) in length; the larvae are released by the female in the late summer.
Size: Length to 7 inches (18 cm).
Range and Habitat: Prince William Sound, Alaska to Punta Gorda, California; around reefs; from 35 to over 100 feet (11 to 31 m).

34. **VERMILION ROCKFISH**   *Sebastes miniatus*
                                                      (Magnificent; vermilion)
Identification: Differs from the other shallow water "red" rockfishes, the canary (35) and yelloweye (36) by having rough scales on the underside of jaw and mottled gray background on body.
Size: Length to 30 inches (76 cm).
Range and Habitat: Vancouver Island, British Columbia to San Benito Islands, Baja California; around reefs; in depths to 900 feet (275 m).

35. **CANARY ROCKFISH**   *Sebastes pinniger*
                                                      (Magnificent; large-finned)
Identification: Canary rockfish lack rough scales on the underside of the jaw (mandible) and the body is yellow-orange and gray in color. Fish smaller than 14 inches (36 cm) have a large black blotch on the spinous dorsal fin.
Natural History: A 21 to 26 inch (53 to 66 cm) female may produce up to 1,900,000 larval rockfish.
Size: Length to 30 inches (76 cm).
Range and Habitat: Cape San Bartolome, Alaska to Cape Colnett, Baja California; around reefs and over soft bottoms; to depths of 900 feet (275 m).

36. **YELLOWEYE ROCKFISH**   *Sebastes ruberrimus*
                                                      (Magnificent; very red)
Identification: The yellow eye and flattened rasp-like spines on the head of adults, and lack of scales on the jaw or on the maxillary are good distinguishing characteristics. Juveniles less than about 14 inches (36 cm) have two silvery-white stripes on sides.
Size: Length to 36 inches (91 cm).
Range and Habitat: Gulf of Alaska to Ensenada, Baja California; around reefs where there are plenty of caves and crevices; in depths from about 50 to 1,200 feet (15 to 366 m).

33. PUGET SOUND ROCKFISH

34. VERMILION ROCKFISH

a) juvenile

35. CANARY ROCKFISH

36. YELLOWEYE ROCKFISH

b) adult

37. **KELP ROCKFISH**   *Sebastes atrovirens*
(Magnificent; black-green)

Identification: Often confused with the grass rockfish (38) but gill rakers on the first arch are long and slender, not short and stubby.
Size: Length to 16.75 inches (43 cm).
Range and Habitat: Timber Cove, California to Punta San Pablo, Baja California; primarily in kelp forests; solitary fish usually observed off bottom near kelp; in depths to 150 feet (46 m).

38. **GRASS ROCKFISH**   *Sebastes rastrelliger*
(Magnificent; rake-bearing)

Identification: Differs from the kelp rockfish (37) by the dark olive-green mottling on the head and body and the 22-25 short, stubby gill rakers on the first gill arch (the only rockfish having this type of gill rakers).
Natural History: Grass rockfish feed on fishes and crabs.
Size: Length to 22 inches (56 cm).
Range and Habitat: Yaquina Bay, Oregon to Playa Maria Bay, Baja California; around eel grass beds and rocky areas with crevices; intertidal out to 150 feet (46 m).

39. **BROWN ROCKFISH**   *Sebastes auriculatus*
(Magnificent; eared)

Identification: The dark brown spot on the rear of the gill cover is very noticeable, also the presence of a coronal spine on the head is a good character if you have the fish in hand.
Size: Length to 21.5 inches (55 cm).
Range and Habitat: Prince William Sound, Alaska to Hipolito Bay, Baja California; around low profile reefs in sandy or silty areas; to depths of 420 feet (128 m).

40. **QUILLBACK ROCKFISH**   *Sebastes maliger*
(Magnificent; mast-bearing)

Identification: Quillback rockfish can be readily recognized by the brown and yellow body color, the brown spots on the anterior ventral portion of the body, and the spinous dorsal fin with deeply notched membranes.
Size: Length to 24 inches (61 cm).
Range and Habitat: Gulf of Alaska to Avila, California and possibly, south to Point Conception; in and around offshore rocky reefs that contain caves and crevices; in depths of about 30 to 900 feet (9 to 274 m).

37. KELP ROCKFISH

38. GRASS ROCKFISH

39. BROWN ROCKFISH

40. QUILLBACK ROCKFISH

43

41.   **CHINA ROCKFISH**   *Sebastes nebulosus*
                                            (Magnificent; clouded)
Identification: The yellow stripe that runs from the front part of the spiny dorsal fin down to the lateral line then posteriorly to the base of the caudal fin and the whitish or yellow spots are good identification characters.
Size: Length to 17 inches (43 cm).
Range and Habitat: Prince William Sound, Alaska to San Miguel Island, California; in and around offshore reefs with crevices and caves; in depths from 10 to 420 feet (3 to 128 m).

42.   **BLACK-AND-YELLOW ROCKFISH**   *Sebastes chrysomelas*
                                            (Magnificent; gold-black)
Identification: The black-and-yellow rockfish is indistinguishable from the gopher rockfish (43) except for the color pattern of large yellow to orange blotches on a black body.
Size: Length to 15.25 inches (39 cm).
Range and Habitat: Eureka, California to Natividad Island, Baja California; around shallow rocky reefs; to depths of 120 feet (37 m).

43.   **GOPHER ROCKFISH**   *Sebastes carnatus*
                                            (Magnificent; flesh-colored)
Identification: Gopher rockfish in contrast to black-and-yellow rockfish (42) have flesh-colored spots and blotches on an olive-brown to brown body.
Size: Length to 15.6 inches (40 cm).
Range and Habitat: Eureka, California to San Roque, Baja California; in and around rocky reefs with caves and crevices; in depths from 10 to 180 feet (3 to 55 m).

44.   **COPPER ROCKFISH**   *Sebastes caurinus*
                                            (Magnificent; northwestern)
Identification: Considered synonymous with whitebelly rockfish, *Sebastes vexillaris*. The copper-brown body with a white area along the posterior two-thirds of the lateral line readily separates the copper rockfish from the brown rockfish (39); also the lack of a coronal spine.
Natural History: Feed on crabs, shrimps, and fishes.
Size: Length to 22.5 inches (57 cm).
Range and Habitat: Kenai Peninsula, Alaska to San Benitos Islands, Baja California; around offshore rocky reefs; in depths from shallow bays to 600 feet (183 m).

41. CHINA ROCKFISH

42. BLACK-AND-YELLOW ROCKFISH

43. GOPHER ROCKFISH

44. COPPER ROCKFISH

45. CALICO ROCKFISH   *Sebastes dalli*
(Magnificent; of Dall, after W. H. Dall, naturalist)

Identification: The calico rockfish can be readily recognized by the slanting brown bars on the light yellow to yellow-green body.

Size: Length to 8 inches (20 cm).

Range and Habitat: San Francisco, California to Rompiente Point, Baja California; around deeper rocky reefs; from 60 to 840 feet (18 to 256 m).

46. HONEYCOMB ROCKFISH   *Sebastes umbrosus*
(Magnificent; shady)

Identification: The honeycomb rockfish has distinctive blackish margins on the scales forming a honeycomb pattern, 3 to 5 white blotches on the back, and white edges on the dorsal, caudal and anal fins. They differ from the freckled rockfish (*S. lentiginosus*, not illustrated), a deep water rockfish, in not having toothed knobs on the premaxillary bones.

Size: Length to 10.5 inches (27 cm); *S. lentiginosus* to 9 inches (23 cm).

Range and Habitat: *S. umbrosus*—Pt. Pinos, Monterey County, California to Pt. San Juanico, Baja California; *S. lentiginosus*—Santa Catalina Island to Los Coronados, Baja California; around bases of offshore rocky reefs; in depths of 90 to 250 feet (27 to 76 m), and 130 to 550 feet (40 to 168 m) respectively.

47. ROSY ROCKFISH   *Sebastes rosaceus*
(Magnificent; rosy)

Identification: The 4 or 5 white blotches on the back have purplish-red borders; this character and the purple bar across the nape will separate the rosy rockfish from the less common, deep-water rosethorn rockfish, (*S. helvomaculatus*, not illustrated), also the rosethorn rockfish has only 16 pectoral rays; the rosy rockfish has 17.

Size: *S. rosaceus*—length to 14.2 inches (37 cm). *S. helvomaculatus*—length to 16 inches (41 cm).

Range and Habitat: *S. rosaceus*—northern California to Turtle Bay, Baja California; *S. helvomaculatus*—Kodiak Island to Point Loma, California. Around offshore rocky reefs usually in caves or crevices; in depths of 50 to 469 feet (15 to 143 m) and 438 to 1,500 feet (134 to 458 m), respectively.

48. STARRY ROCKFISH   *Sebastes constellatus*
(Magnificent; starry)

Identification: Starry rockfish also have 4 or 5 whitish blotches on the back; these, plus numerous small white spots that cover the body are good identification characters.

Size: Length to 18 inches (46 cm).

Range and Habitat: San Francisco, California to Thetis Bank, Baja California; around offshore rocky reefs with caves and crevices; in depths of 65 to 540 feet (20 to 165 m).

45. CALICO ROCKFISH

46. HONEYCOMB ROCKFISH

47. ROSY ROCKFISH

48. STARRY ROCKFISH

49. **TREEFISH**   *Sebastes serriceps*

(Magnificent; saw-head)

Identification: The treefish is best identified by the black bars on the olive-yellow body and the red lips.

Size: Length to 16 inches (41 cm).

Range and Habitat: San Francisco, California, to Cedros Island, Baja California; around rocky reefs with caves and crevices; in shallow depths out to 150 feet (46 m).

50. **TIGER ROCKFISH**   *Sebastes nigrocinctus*

(Magnificent; black-banded)

Identification: The distinctive body color of light pink to red, with five vertical dark red to black bars, separates this rockfish from all others.

Natural History: Tiger rockfish are very cryptic and usually are shy of divers; however, they can be very aggressive in defending their territory.

Size: Length to 24 inches (61 cm).

Range and Habitat: Prince William Sound, Alaska to Point Buchon, California; in crevices and caves; in depths from about 80 to 900 feet (24 to 274 m).

51. **FLAG ROCKFISH**   *Sebastes rubrivinctus*

(Magnificent; red-banded)

Identification: Flag rockfish are often confused with the deep water redbanded rockfish (*S. babcocki*, not illustrated) but there is a difference in the vertical red bands. *S. rubrivinctus'* first band angles anteriorly from the first dorsal spine down across the rear of the gill cover, while the band on *S. babcocki* angles posteriorily across the upper edge of the gill cover and ends on the pectoral fin.

Size: *S. rubrivinctus*—length to about 15 inches (38 cm). *S. babcocki*—length to 25 inches (64 cm).

Range and Habitat: *S. rubrivinctus*—San Francisco to San Quintin, Baja California. *S. babcocki*—Amchitka, Alaska to San Diego, California. Around offshore reefs; from 100 to 600 feet (31 to 183 m), and 900 to 1,560 feet (274 to 476 m), respectively.

FAMILY HEXAGRAMMIDAE

52. **KELP GREENLING**   *Hexagrammos decagrammus*

(Six-line; ten-line)

Identification: Kelp greenling have two pairs of cirri, one over the eyes and the other smaller pair is located between the eyes and the origin of the dorsal fin (occasionally the second pair is absent). The cirri over the eyes are never more than 3/4 the diameter of the eye. The interior of the mouth is usually yellowish.

Size: Length to 21 inches (53 cm).

Range and Habitat: Aleutian Islands, Alaska to La Jolla, California; around rocky reefs and in kelp beds; from the intertidal to 150 feet (46 m).

49. TREEFISH

50. TIGER ROCKFISH

a) female

51. FLAG ROCKFISH

52. KELP GREENLING   b) male

53.   WHITESPOTTED GREENLING   *Hexagrammos stelleri*
(Six-line; of Steller, for G. W. Steller, 18th century naturalist)
Identification: The white spots, single pair of cirri over eyes, and the short 4th lateral line, which does not extend posteriorly beyond origin of the anal fin, are all good characters for identifying this fish.
Size: Length to 19 inches (48 cm).
Range and Habitat: Japan to Puget Sound, Washington; around shallow reefs and kelp beds.

54.   ROCK GREENLING   *Hexagrammos superciliosus*
(Six-line; eyebrow)
Identification: Rock greenlings have blue mouths and a single pair of large cirri over the eyes, each cirri will be more than 3/4 diameter of eye.
Size: Length to 24 inches (61 cm).
Range and Habitat: Bering Sea to Point Conception, California; around shallow rocky reefs and kelp beds.

55.   LINGCOD   *Ophiodon elongatus*
(Elongated ↔ snake-tooth)
Identification: Lingcod have only one lateral line and they are the only member of the family that have a large mouth and large canine teeth, the maxillary extends to at least the middle of the eye.
Natural History: Males guard eggs until they hatch; lingcod feed on fishes, squids and octopus.
Size: Weight reported to 105 pounds (48 kg).
Range and Habitat: Kodiak Island and Prince William Sound, Alaska to Point San Carlos, Baja California; around rock reefs, juveniles on sand and mud bottom; from shallow bays to depths of 1,400 feet (427 m).

56.   PAINTED GREENLING   *Oxylebius pictus*
(Painted ↔ sharp fish)
Identification: Painted greenling also possess only one lateral line; they differ from the other members of the family in having a very small mouth, the end of the maxillary does not reach the eye.
Size: Length to 10 inches (25 cm).
Range and Habitat: Queen Charlotte Islands, British Columbia to Point San Carlos, Baja California; around rocky reefs; from the intertidal to depths of 160 feet (49 m).

53. WHITESPOTTED GREENLING

54. ROCK GREENLING

55. LINGCOD

56. PAINTED GREENLING

FAMILY COTTIDAE

57.   CABEZON   *Scorpaenichthys marmoratus*
                                                     (Like Scorpaena fish; marbled)
Identification: Cabezon have no scales on their bodies, they have a large cirrus over each eye and a single cirrus on the snout.
Natural History: Feed on molluscs, such as squids, octopus and abalone. Males guard eggs.
Size: Length to 39 inches (99 cm).
Range and Habitat: Sitka, Alaska to Point Abreojos, Baja California; around rocky reefs; from the intertidal to depths of 250 feet (75 m).

58.   GREAT SCULPIN   *Myoxocephalus polyacanthocephalus*
                                     (Dormouse head; many spine head)
Identification: There are at least three species of *Myoxocephalus* reported from the Gulf of Alaska and southeastern Alaska. The great sculpin is apparently the largest and possesses a long, straight, smooth upper opercular spine and scales embedded in fleshy papillae on head.
Size: Length to 30 inches (76 cm).
Range and Habitat: Japan and Bering Sea to Washington; on soft bottoms and around reefs; from the intertidal to depths of 126 feet (38 m).

59.   LONGFIN SCULPIN   *Jordania zonope*
                (Jordan, after David Starr Jordan, ichthyologist; zone window)
Identification: The only sculpin in our area with three black vertical bars below the eye and 17 to 18 spines in the dorsal fin.
Size: Length to 5.1 inches (13 cm).
Range and Habitat: Prince William Sound, Alaska to Avila, California; in and around caves and crevices; from the intertidal to 126 feet (38 m).

60.   BROWN IRISH LORD   *Hemilepidotus spinosus*
                                                    (Half-scaled; spiny)
Identification: Brown Irish lords are very difficult to distinguish from the red Irish lord (61) underwater. If you have the fish in hand count the scale rows below the dorsal fin, if it has 7 to 8 rows it is a brown Irish lord.
Size: Length to 11.3 inches (29 cm).
Range and Habitat: Prince William Sound, Alaska to Santa Barbara, California; around reefs; from the intertidal to depths of 252 feet (77 m).

57. CABEZON

58. GREAT SCULPIN

59. LONGFIN SCULPIN

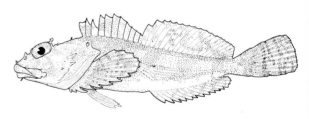

60. BROWN IRISH LORD

61. RED IRISH LORD *Hemilepidotus hemilepidotus*
(Half-scaled; half-scaled)

Identification: Red Irish lords have only 4 or 5 rows of scales below the dorsal fin and several patches of red on the upper body.
Size: Length to 20 inches (51 cm).
Range and Habitat: Sea of Okhotsk to Monterey, California; on rocky reefs; in depths from the intertidal to 156 feet (48 m).

62. SAILFIN SCULPIN *Nautichthys oculofasciatus*
(Eye-banded ←→ sailor fish)

Identification: This nocturnal sculpin is readily identified by the high spinous dorsal fin and the dark vertical band that runs through the eye.
Size: Length to 6.8 inches (17 cm).
Range and Habitat: Eastern Kamchatka and Prince William Sound, Alaska to San Miguel Island, California; around rocky reefs; from the intertidal to depths of 360 feet (110 m).

63. GRUNT SCULPIN *Rhamphocottus richardsoni*
(Richardson's after John Richardson, naturalist ←→ snout cottus)

Identification: This distinctive sculpin can be identified by the snout, about twice the length of the maxillary, and the free, lowermost pectoral rays.
Size: Length to 3.3 inches (8 cm).
Range and Habitat: Bering Sea to Santa Monica Bay, California; on rocky reefs; from the intertidal to depths of 540 feet (165 m).

64. BUFFALO SCULPIN *Enophrys bison*
(On eyebrow; bison)

Identification: Buffalo sculpin have a single long preopercular spine, bony plates on the lateral line and 8 to 10 anal soft-rays.
Size: Length to 14.6 inches (37 cm).
Range and Habitat: Kodiak Island, Alaska to Monterey, California; around shallow reefs.

61. RED IRISH LORD

62. SAILFIN SCULPIN

63. GRUNT SCULPIN

64. BUFFALO SCULPIN

65.   **SNUBNOSE SCULPIN**   *Orthonopias triacis*

(Straight eyes; three points)

Identification: The snubnose and the location of the anus much closer to the base of the pelvic fins than to the anal fin separates this common sculpin from all others.
Size: Length to 4 inches (10 cm).
Range and Habitat: Monterey, California to San Geronimo Island, Baja California; around rocky areas; intertidal to depths of 100 feet (30 m).

66.   **CORALLINE SCULPIN**   *Artedius corallinus*

(Artedi's after Petrus Artedi, ichthyologist; corralline algae, the fishes habitat)

Identification: Very similar to *Artedius lateralis* (not illustrated), the smoothhead sculpin. The only way to separate the two is by examination with a hand lens; the coralline sculpin has 39 to 49 oblique rows of scales, and 10 to 18 scales in largest row, while the smoothhead sculpin has only 18 to 29 oblique rows of scales and 3 to 11 scales in longest row.
Size: Length to 5.5 inches (14 cm); *A. lateralis*, length to 5.2 inches (13 cm).
Range and Habitat: *A. corallinus*—Orcas Island, Washington to San Martin Island, Baja California; *A. lateralis*—USSR to Sulfer Point, San Quintin, Baja California; around rocky reefs; in depths from intertidal to 70 feet and 25 feet (21 and 8 m) respectively.

67.   **LAVENDER SCULPIN**   *Leiocottus hirundo*

(Smooth cottus; swallow)

Identification: The distinctive blue spots on the dorsal fin, red bands on the sides of the body and the long first dorsal spine which is about twice as long as the 3rd dorsal spine, should separate this fish from other sculpins.
Size: Length to 10 inches (25 cm).
Range and Habitat: Point Conception, California* to Point Banda, Baja California; on sand and rock bottoms around kelp beds; in depths from the intertidal to 120 feet (37 m).

FAMILY AGONIDAE

68.   **STURGEON POACHER**   *Agonus acipenserinus*

(Without joints; like a sturgeon)

Identification: The sturgeon poacher is the only poacher with clusters of yellow cirri under the snout. Poachers are readily recognized by the presence of body plates instead of scales.
Size: Length to 12 inches (30 m).
Range and Habitat: Bering Sea to Eureka, California; on soft bottoms and around reefs; in depths from about 10 to 180 feet (3 to 55 m).

65. SNUBNOSE SCULPIN

66. CORALLINE SCULPIN

67. LAVENDER SCULPIN

68. STURGEON POACHER

FAMILY SERRANIDAE

69. GIANT SEA BASS

Stereolepis gigas
(Giant ←→firm scale)

Identification: This increasingly rare fish is distinguished by having two spines on the gill cover rather than three as in the other sea basses. Juveniles and young adults have black spots on the sides; these spots may fade in large adults.

Natural History: May live to over 100 years of age; a 435 lb. individual was determined to be about 75 years old.

Size: Length to 7 feet (213 cm) and weight to 557 lbs. (253 kg).

Range and Habitat: Humboldt Bay, California to the Gulf of California; around rocky reefs; in depths from 18 to 100 feet (5 to 30 m).

70. KELP BASS

Paralabrax clathratus
(Related to the sea bass; latticed)

Identification: The kelp bass has a third dorsal spine that is about the same length as the fourth and fifth spines. The white blotches between the dorsal fin and lateral line are also distinctive. Old fish have orange-yellow chins.

Size: Length to 28.4 inches (72 cm).

Range and Habitat: Columbia River to Magdalena Bay, Baja California; around reefs and kelp beds; from the surface to depths of 150 feet (46 m).

71. SPOTTED SAND BASS

Paralabrax maculatofasiatus
(Related to the sea bass; spotted and banded)

Identification: The spotted sand bass has black spots on the upper body and the third dorsal fin spine is longer than the fourth or fifth spine.

Size: Length to 22 inches (56 cm).

Range and Habitat: Monterey, California to Mazatlan, Mexico, including the Gulf of California; on sand and around reefs; to depths of 150 feet (46 m).

72. BARRED SAND BASS

Paralabrax nebulifer
(Related to the sea bass; cloud bearing)

Identification: The barred sand bass is similar to the spotted sand bass, except that barred sand bass lack the black spots on the body. The third dorsal fin spine is longer than the fourth or fifth spine.

Size: Length to 25.6 inches (65 cm).

Range and Habitat: Santa Cruz, California to Magdalena Bay, Baja California; on sand bottoms and around reefs; to depths of 600 feet (183 m).

K. Lucas

69. GIANT SEA BASS

70. KELP BASS

71. SPOTTED SAND BASS

72. BARRED SAND BASS

FAMILY MALACANTHIDAE

73. OCEAN WHITEFISH — *Caulolatilus princeps*

(Like *Latilus* a closely related genus having few fin rays; leader)

Identification: Ocean whitefish might be confused with yellowtail, *Seriola dorsalis* [Family Carangidae (not illustrated)] but their long continuous dorsal fin is of a uniform height and they lack the yellow stripe on the sides of the yellowtail.

Size: Length to 40 inches (102 cm).

Range and Habitat: Vancouver Island, British Columbia to Peru; on soft bottoms and around reefs; to depths of 300 feet (92 m).

FAMILY CARANGIDAE

74. JACK MACKEREL — *Trachurus symmetricus*

(Rough tail; symmetrical)

Identification: This pelagic schooling jack differs from the other species that occur in our area by having a lateral line with a dorsal branch and 40 to 55 enlarged shields on the median lateral line.

Size: Length to 32 inches (81 cm).

Range and Habitat: Southeastern Alaska to the Galapagos Islands; in surface waters around reefs and kelp beds and in open ocean; to depths of 150 feet (46 m).

FAMILY HAEMULIDAE

75. SALEMA — *Xenistius californiensis*

(California ←→ strange sail)

Identification: This member of the grunt family can be distinguished by the 6 to 8 horizontal orange-brown stripes on the sides and the large eye.

Size: Length to 10 inches (25 cm).

Range and Habitat: Monterey Bay, California to Peru, including the Gulf of California; in aggregations over sandy and rocky shallows and in sheltered bays; in depths from 4 to 35 feet (1 to 11 m).

76. SARGO — *Anisotremus davidsonii*

(Davidson's after George Davidson, astronomer ←→ Unequal aperture)

Identification: This grunt can be identified by the single black bar that extends down the sides from the base of the dorsal fin and passes under the pectoral fin. The 9 to 11 soft-rays in the anal fin distinguish the sargo from members of the surfperch family (Embiotocidae) which have fewer than 13 anal soft-rays.

Size: Length to 17.4 inches (44 cm).

Range and Habitat: Santa Cruz, California to Magdalena Bay, Baja California and the upper Gulf of California; around reefs and kelp beds; to depths of 130 feet (40 m).

73. OCEAN WHITEFISH

74. JACK MACKEREL

75. SALEMA

76. SARGO

FAMILY SCIAENIDAE

77. YELLOWFIN CROAKER

Umbrina roncador
(Shady; croaker)

Identification: There are 10 species of croakers recorded from our area. The yellow-fin croaker can be distinguished from the others by the yellowish fins, dark oblique wavy lines on sides of body, small barbel on the chin, and the 2 spines in the anal fin.
Size: Length to 20.1 inches (51 cm).
Range and Habitat: Point Conception, California to the Gulf of California; around kelp beds and over soft bottoms; from surf zone to depths of 150 feet (46 m).

78. BLACK CROAKER

Cheilotrema saturnam
(Lip-pore; dusky)

Identification: Black croakers, as the name implies, are blackish with coppery tints or purplish-bronze in color; they differ from the other croakers in the lack of a chin whisker and having 25 to 28 dorsal soft-rays.
Size: Length to 15 inches (38 cm).
Range and Habitat: Point Conception, California to Magdalena Bay, Baja California; in rocky crevices and caves during daylight, come out to feed at night; to depths of 150 feet (46 m).

FAMILY KYPHOSIDAE

79. OPALEYE

Girella nigricans
(A small wrasse; blackish)

Identification: Opaleye usually have 1 or 2 whitish spots on the back and blue opalescent eyes.
Natural History: Opaleye feed on a variety of algae in order to obtain the animals that live on the algae.
Size: Length to 25.4 inches (64 cm).
Range and Habitat: San Francisco, California to Cape San Lucas, Baja California; around shallow reefs and kelp beds; from the intertidal to depths of 95 feet (29 m).

80. ZEBRAPERCH

Hermosilla azurea
(Capital city of the state of Sonora, Mexico; sky-blue)

Identification: Zebraperch have nine or ten dark vertical bars on their sides, a bright blue spot on the operculum and a sheath of scales along the base of the dorsal fin.
Size: Length to 17.4 inches (44 cm).
Range and Habitat: Monterey, California to the Gulf of California; around kelp beds and off sand and rocky bottoms; from the intertidal to depths of 25 feet (8 m).

77.   YELLOWFIN CROAKER

78.   BLACK CROAKER

79.   OPALEYE

80.   ZEBRAPERCH

81. **HALFMOON**   *Medialuna californiensis*
                                                  (California ↔ half-moon)
Identification: The halfmoon's distinctive half-moon shaped tail, overall gray-blue body and the sheath of scales covering the soft dorsal and anal fins, separate them from all other members of the family.
Size: Length to 19 inches (48 cm).
Range and Habitat: Klamath River, California to the Gulf of California; around reefs and kelp beds; to depths of 130 feet (40 m).

82. **STRIPED SEA CHUB**   *Kyphosus analogus*
                                                  (Hump; analogous)
Identification: The striped sea chub is similar to the zebraperch in that they have fewer than 15 dorsal soft-rays; they lack the vertical bars on the sides; instead there are dark spots on the scales which appear as longitudinal stripes.
Size: Length to 18 inches (46 cm).
Range and Habitat: Oceanside, California to Peru including the Gulf of California; around shallow kelp beds and rocky areas.

FAMILY CHAETODONTIDAE
83. **SCYTHEMARKED BUTTERFLYFISH**   *Chaetodon falcifer*
                                          (Bristle tooth; scythe bearer)
Identification: The distinctive black scythe mark on the sides is the best character for recognition.
Size: Length to about 6 inches (15 cm).
Range and Habitat: Santa Catalina Island to Galapagos Islands, common around San Benitos Islands, Baja California; around rocky and coral reefs; to depths of 492 feet (150 m).

FAMILY EMBIOTOCIDAE
84. **RUBBERLIP SURFPERCH**   *Rhacochilus toxotes*
                                  (Rag lip; toxotes, an East Indian archerfish)
Identification: The large fleshy lips of this surfperch have two ventral lobes, and the 1st ray in the soft rayed portion of the dorsal fin is shorter than the 3rd ray; these characters plus the brassy overtones on the brown body should confirm your identification.
Natural History: All members of this family are viviparous, that is the embryonic surfperch develop within the female's body and receive nourishment from the female.
Size: Length to 18.5 inches (47 cm).
Range and Habitat: Russian Gulch State Beach, California to Thurloe Head, Baja California; around reefs, kelp beds and piers; from shallow bays to depths of 150 feet (46 m).

81. HALFMOON

82. STRIPED SEA CHUB

83. SCYTHEMARKED BUTTERFLYFISH

84. RUBBERLIP SURFPERCH

85. PILE SURFPERCH

Damalichthys vacca
(Calf-fish; cow)

Identification: Pile surfperch have very long dorsal soft rays, the longest is about twice the length of the longest dorsal spine. The dark bar on the silvery gray sides is also very distinctive.
Size: Length to 17.4 inches (44 cm).
Range and Habitat: Port Wrangell, Alaska to Guadalupe Island, Baja California; around reefs, kelp beds and piers; from shallow bays to depths of 240 feet (74 m).

86. WHITE SURFPERCH

Phanerodon furcatus
(Evident tooth; forked)

Identification: White surfperch have white pelvic fins, a thin black line at base of the soft-rayed dorsal fin and the dorsal soft-rays are only slightly longer than the longest dorsal spine.
Size: Length to 13.3 inches (34 cm*).
Range and Habitat: Vancouver, British Columbia to Point Cabras, Baja California; around reefs and in kelp beds; from shallow bays to depths of 140 feet (43 m).

87. SHARPNOSE SURFPERCH

Phanerodon atripes
(Evident tooth; black foot)

Identification: The reddish speckles on the scales along the sides and black tipped pelvic fins distinguish the sharpnose surfperch from the white surfperch (86).
Natural History: Sharpnose surfperch occasionally function as "cleaners;" they have been observed picking parasites from molas (126), blue rockfish (27) and blacksmith (95).
Size: Length to 11.5 inches (29 cm).
Range and Habitat: Bodega Bay, California to San Benito Islands, Baja California; around deep reefs, kelp beds and on occasion, shallow reefs and piers, to depths of 750 feet (229 m).

88. WALLEYE SURFPERCH

Hyperprosopon argenteum
(Above-face; silvery)

Identification: The walleye surfperch can be separated from the other members of the genus *Hyperprosopon* (not illustrated) by the following: If the fish has black tipped pelvic fins and a black edge on tail, it is the walleye surfperch; if it has black blotches in the spinous dorsal and soft anal fin it is the spotfin surfperch, *H. anale*; if the fish lacks any black markings on the fins it is the silver surfperch, *H. ellipticum*.
Size: *H. argenteum*, length to 12 inches (30 cm); *H. anale*, 6 inches (15 cm); *H. ellipticum*, 10.5 inches (27 cm).
Range and Habitat: *H. argenteum*; Vancouver Island, B.C. to San Benito Islands,* Baja California. *H. anale*; Seal Rock, Oregon to Blanca Bay, Baja California. *H. ellipticum*; Vancouver Island, B.C. to Rio San Vicente, Baja California. All three in surf and/or soft bottoms and *H. argenteum* around kelp beds and reefs to depths of 60, 210, and 360 feet (18, 64, 110 m), respectively.

85. PILE SURFPERCH

86. WHITE SURFPERCH

87. SHARPNOSE SURFPERCH

88. WALLEYE SURFPERCH

89. BLACK SURFPERCH   *Embiotoca jacksoni*

(Jackson's, after A.C. Jackson who discovered
this family's viviparity ➝ viviparous)

Identification: This dark surfperch has a patch of enlarged scales between the pectoral fin and pelvic fin, yellow-orange lips, a blue bar at the base of the anal fin and several dark bars on sides.

Size: Length to 15.4 inches (39 cm).

Range and Habitat: Fort Bragg, California to Point Abreojos, Baja California; around reefs and kelp beds; from shallow bays to depths of 130 feet (40 m).

90. STRIPED SURFPERCH   *Embiotoca lateralis*

(Viviparous; lateral; pertaining to the side)

Identification: Striped surfperch can best be distinguished from the similar rainbow surfperch (91) by the dusky pelvic fins and 29-33 soft rays in the anal fin.

Size: Length to 15 inches (38 cm).

Range and Habitat: Port Wrangell, Alaska to Point Cabras, Baja California; around reefs, piers and kelp beds, from shallow bays to depths of 55 feet (17 m).

91. RAINBOW SURFPERCH   *Hypsurus caryi*

(Cary's, after T. C. Cary, discoverer of this fish; high tail)

Identification: The rainbow surfperch has bright blue and red-orange pelvic fins and only 20-24 anal soft-rays. These characters and the reddish vertical bars on the sides distinguish it from the striped surfperch (90).

Size: Length to 12 inches (30 cm).

Range and Habitat: Cape Mendocino, California to San Martin Island*, Baja California; around reefs, piers and kelp beds; from shallow bays to depths of 130 feet (40 m).

92. SHINER SURFPERCH   *Cymatogaster aggregata*

(Fetus belly; crowded together)

Identification: These small silvery surfperch have 3 vertical yellow bars on sides. Males during breeding season have black striping which tends to cover yellow bars.

Size: Length to 7.6 inches (19.3 cm).

Range and Habitat: Port Wrangell, Alaska to San Quintin Bay, Baja California; around piers, reefs, kelp beds and on soft bottoms; from shallow bays to depths of 480 feet (146 m).

89. BLACK SURFPERCH

90. STRIPED SURFPERCH

91. RAINBOW SURFPERCH

92. SHINER SURFPERCH

93. **KELP SURFPERCH**   *Brachyistius frenatus*
                                                 (Short dorsal fin; bridled)
Identification: Kelp surfperch can be separated from shiner surfperch (92) by their lack of the yellow bars on the body and they have only 13 to 16 soft-rays in the dorsal fin.
Natural History: Kelp surfperch are "cleaners."
Size: Length to 8.5 inches (22 cm).
Range and Habitat: Vancouver Island, British Columbia to Turtle Bay, Baja California; in kelp beds; from surface to depths of 100 feet (31 m).

FAMILY POMACENTRIDAE

94. **GARIBALDI**   *Hypsypops rubicundus*
                                                 (High below eye; red)
Identification: The garibaldi's distinctive bright orange color separates it from all other fish in our area. Juveniles have iridescent blue spots on the body.
Size: Length to 14 inches (36 cm).
Range and Habitat: Monterey Bay, California to Magdalena Bay, Baja California, rare north of Point Conception; around reefs and kelp beds; to depths of 95 feet (29 m).
Note: The garibaldi is the only marine fish in California that is completely protected by law.

95. **BLACKSMITH**   *Chromis punctipinnis*
                                                 (Spot fin ←→ chromis)
Identification: This dark blue damselfish has black spots on the body, dorsal fin and on the tail.
Natural History: Blacksmiths are major "customers of the cleaners" particularly senorita (98).
Size: Length to 12 inches (30 cm).
Range and Habitat: Monterey, California to Point San Pablo, Baja California; around reefs and kelp beds; to depths of 270 feet* (82 m).

FAMILY SPHYRAENIDAE

96. **CALIFORNIA BARRACUDA**   *Sphyraena argentea*
                                                 (Silvery ←→ hammer)
Identification: The California barracuda is distinguished by having numerous large canine teeth and two widely spaced dorsal fins.
Natural History: A female may release 500,000 pelagic eggs.
Size: Length to 48 inches (122 cm). Weight to 18 lbs. (8 kg).
Range and Habitat: Prince William Sound, Alaska to Cape San Lucas, Baja California; pelagic, to depths of 60 feet (18 m).

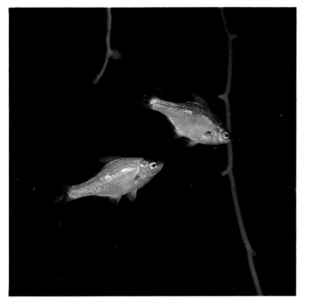

93. KELP SURFPERCH

a) juvenile

94. GARIBALDI
b) adult

95. BLACKSMITH

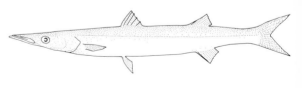

96. CALIFORNIA BARRACUDA

FAMILY LABRIDAE

97.   CALIFORNIA SHEEPHEAD
Semicossyphus pulcher

(One-half of a related species; beautiful)

Identification: Both sexes of California sheephead have large doglike teeth and white chins. Juveniles have 7 black blotches of which 5 are visible from the side on the fins and base of tail.

Natural History: Sheephead are hermaphroditic; when sexually mature they are females, but after a few years almost all will become males for the remainder of their lives.

Size: Length to 36 inches (91 cm).

Range and Habitat: Monterey to Cape San Lucas, Baja California, and an isolated population in the northern Gulf of California; around reefs and in kelp beds; to depths of 289 feet (88 m).

98.   SENORITA
Oxyjulis californica

(California ⟷ sharp *julis*, another species of wrasse)

Identification: The only dusky orange, cigar-shaped wrasse with large scales and a black spot on the tail fin in our area.

Natural History: The most common "cleaner" in California.

Size: Length to 10 inches (25 cm).

Range and Habitat: Salt Point, Sonoma County, California to Cedros Island, Baja California; around reefs and in kelp beds; to depths of 331 feet* (101 m).

99.   ROCK WRASSE
Halichoeres semicinctus

(Half-banded ⟷ pig-of-the-sea)

Identification: Rock wrasse have a lateral line that has an abrupt arch beneath posterior portion of the dorsal fin. Males have a dark blue bar near base of pectoral fin. Adults have red eyes. Juveniles have dark stripes on sides.

Natural History: Like California sheephead, rock wrasse are also hermaphroditic. Females change into males at about 5 years of age.

Size: Length to 15 inches (38 cm).

Range and Habitat: Point Conception to Gulf of California; around reefs and in kelp beds; to depths of 78 feet (24 m).

a) juvenile

b) female

97. CALIFORNIA SHEEPHEAD   c) male

98. SENORITA

99. ROCK WRASSE   a) female   b) male

FAMILY BATHYMASTERIDAE

100. SMOOTH RONQUIL — *Rathbunella hypoplecta*

(Rathbun, for U.S. Fish Commissioner R. Rathbun; folded underneath)

Identification: The smooth ronquil has 15 unbranched soft rays in the the anterior dorsal fin, the remaining posterior dorsal soft-rays are branched. The fin rays are pigmented and there is a greenish blotch at the base of the pectoral fin.

Size: Length to 8.5 inches (22 cm).

Range and Habitat: Pacific Northwest to northern Baja California; on sand and rocky bottoms, usually at the base of reefs; to depths of at least 100 feet (31 m).

101. NORTHERN RONQUIL — *Ronquilus jordani*

(Jordan's, for David Starr Jordan, discoverer of this fish ↠ one who grunts)

Identification: The first 20 to 30 soft rays in the dorsal fin are unbranched in this ronquil; they also have orange stripes below the eye and on the lower posterior portion of the body.

Size: Length to 7.1 inches (18 cm).

Range and Habitat: Bering Sea to Monterey Bay, California; on sand and rocky substrate; in depths from 60 to 540 feet (18-165 m).

102. ALASKAN RONQUIL — *Bathymaster caeruleofasciatus*

(Deep searcher; blue-banded)

Identification: The Alaskan ronquil has only 3 or 4 unbranched soft rays on the first part of the dorsal fin. In addition the Alaskan ronquil differs from other members of the genus *Bathymaster* by having scales on the inner rays of the pelvic fin and on the caudal fin for more than 1/2 of its length and the maxillary extends to or past the posterior edge of the eye.

Size: Length to about 12 inches (30 cm).

Range and Habitat: Sea of Okhotsk and Bering Sea to southeastern Alaska; on rocky bottoms in crevices and caves; to depths of about 100 feet (31 m).

FAMILY ANARHICHADIDAE

103. WOLF-EEL — *Anarrhichthys ocellatus*

(Anarhichas fish, ancient name for a related species; eye-like spots)

Identification: Wolf-eels lack pelvic fins and possess large, strong canine and molar teeth.

Natural History: Wolf-eels feed on crabs, urchins and other hard shelled invertebrates.

Size: Length to 80 inches (203 cm).

Range and Habitat: Sea of Japan and Kodiak Island to Imperial Beach, San Diego County, California; in and around reefs with crevices and caves; to depths of 738 feet (225 m).

100. SMOOTH RONQUIL

101. NORTHERN RONQUIL

102. ALASKAN RONQUIL

103. WOLF-EEL

FAMILY BLENNIDAE

104. BAY BLENNY
Hypsoblennius gentilis
(High *Blennius*; related)

Identification: Bay blennies have a serrated flap (cirrus) above each eye that is not divided or branched at base.

Size: Length to 5.8 inches (15 cm).

Range and Habitat: Monterey to Gulf of California; in crevices around reefs in bays; to depths of 80 feet (24 m).

FAMILY CLINIDAE

105. ONESPOT FRINGEHEAD
Neoclinus uninotatus
(One-marked, in reference to single dorsal ocellus ⟶new clinus)

Identification: The largest cirrus above each eye is larger than the diameter of the eye and the single ocellus in the anterior dorsal fin are good characters to distinguish this fringehead.

Size: Length to 9 inches (23 cm).

Range and Habitat: Bodega Bay to San Diego, California; in holes and crevices on soft and rocky bottoms; in depths from 10 to 90 feet (3-27 m).

106. SARCASTIC FRINGEHEAD
Neoclinus blanchardi
(Blanchard's, after S. B. Blanchard, discoverer of this fish ⟶new clinus)

Identification: Sarcastic fringeheads have two ocelli in the dorsal fin, one between the 1st and 2nd spines and the other between the 5th and 9th spines; also the maxillary extends almost to the back edge of the gill cover. None of the cirri over the eyes is larger than the diameter of the eye.

Size: Length to 12 inches (30 cm).

Range and Habitat: San Francisco, California to Cedros Island, Baja California; in holes and crevices on soft and rocky bottoms; in depths from 10 to 200 feet (3-61 m).

107. ISLAND KELPFISH
Alloclinus holderi
(Holder's, after naturalist C. H. Holder ⟶different clinus)

Identification: Island kelpfish have very long pectoral fins, extending at least to the origin of the anal fin. The lateral line descends abruptly at about mid-body.

Size: Length to 4 inches (10 cm).

Range and Habitat: Santa Cruz Island, California to Point San Pablo, Baja California; around rocky areas; to depths of 162 feet (50 m).

D. Behrens

104. BAY BLENNY

105. ONESPOT FRINGEHEAD

106. SARCASTIC FRINGEHEAD

107. ISLAND KELPFISH

108. GIANT KELPFISH
Heterostichus rostratus

(Long-nosed ←→ different rank)

Identification: The giant kelpfish is the only member of the family in our area with a forked tail. The color is highly variable and usually matches the kelp or algae in the vicinity.

Size: Length to 24 inches (61 cm).

Range and Habitat: British Columbia to Cape San Lucas, Baja California; around algae and kelp; to depths of 132 feet (40 m).

109. KELPFISH
Gibbonsia spp.

(Gibbons, after W. P. Gibbons, early California Academy of Sciences naturalist)

Identification: There are only four species of *Gibbonsia* in our area. They are difficult to separate without the use of a microscope: If the dorsal soft-rays are evenly spaced it is the striped kelpfish, *G. metzi*; if the posterior dorsal soft rays have wider spacing than the anterior rays, and there are scales on the caudal fin, it is the spotted kelpfish, *G. elegans*; if there are no scales on the caudal peduncle or tail, it is the crevice kelpfish, *G. montereyensis*; if there are no scales on the caudal fin but there are scales on the caudal peduncle, it is the scarlet kelpfish, *G. erythra*.

Size: *G. metzi, G. elegans, G. montereyensis,* and *G. erythra* lengths to 9.2, 6.2, 4.4, and 6.0 inches respectively (23, 16, 11 and 15 cm).

Range and Habitat: *G. metzi*, Vancouver Island, British Columbia to Point Rompiente, Baja California; *G. elegans*, Point Piedras Blancas, California to Magadalena Bay, Baja California; *G. montereyensis*, British Columbia to Rio Santo Tomas, Baja California; *G. erythra*, Santa Cruz Island, California to Point Banda, Baja California. All on reefs with algae or kelp; to depths of 30, 185, 25, 120 feet respectively (9, 57, 8 and 37 m).

FAMILY STICHAEIDAE

110. MONKEYFACE-EEL
Cebidichthys violaceus

(Violet ←→ monkey fish)

Identification: The monkeyface-eel has a high, fleshy ridge with two bumps on top of the head and two dark bars radiating posteriorly from the eyes. They also lack pelvic fins.

Size: Length to 30 inches (76 cm).

Range and Habitat: Brookings, Oregon to San Quintin Bay, Baja California; in crevices and holes in rocky areas; to depths of 80 feet (24 m).

111. MOSSHEAD WARBONNET
Chirolophis nugator

(Hand crest; elegant appearance)

Identification: This distinctive fish has 12 to 13 eye spots or ocelli along the dorsal fin and a dense cluster of cirri on the head. These characters separate it from the decorated warbonnet, *C. decoratus* (not illustrated), which has a large complex cirrus, the length exceeds the diameter of the eye, in front of each eye and cirri on the first four or five dorsal fin spines.

Size: *C. nugator*, length to 5.6 inches (14 cm); *C. decoratus*, length to 16.5 inches (42 cm).

Range and Habitat: *C. nugator*, Prince William Sound, Alaska to San Miguel Island, California; *C. decoratus*, Bering Sea to Humboldt Bay, California; in crevices around rocky areas; to 264 feet and from 60 to 300 feet respectively (81 and 18-92 m).

108. GIANT KELPFISH

109. KELPFISH

L. Barr

110. MONKEYFACE-EEL

111. MOSSHEAD WARBONNET

FAMILY GOBIIDAE

112. BLACKEYE GOBY — *Coryphopterus nicholsii*

(Nichol's, after Captain H. E. Nichols, U.S.N., discoverer of this fish ←→ head fin)
Identification: Blackeye gobies have an iridescent blue spot beneath each eye, pelvic fins that reach anus and a black area on outer edge of first dorsal fin.
Size: Length to 6 inches (15 cm).
Range and Habitat: Queen Charlotte Island, British Columbia to Point Rompiente, Baja California; on sand, mud and rock bottoms; to depths of 420 feet (126 m).

113. BLUEBANDED GOBY — *Lythrypnus dalli*

(Dall's, after W. H. Dall, discoverer of this fish ←→ red sleeper)
Identification: This bright red fish has 2 to 6 bright blue vertical bands on the body and 12 to 14 soft-rays in the anal fin.
Size: Length to 2.2 inches (6 cm).
Range and Habitat: Morro Bay, California to Gulf of California, in and around crevices on rocky substrate; to depths of 210 feet (64 m).

114. ZEBRA GOBY — *Lythrypnus zebra*

(Zebra ←→ red sleeper)
Identification: The zebra goby's body is more orange than red. They have 12 to 16 vertical blue bands and only 9 soft-rays in the anal fin.
Size: Length to 2.2 inches (6 cm).
Range and Habitat: Carmel Bay, California to Clarion Island, Mexico; in holes and crevices, around rocky reefs; to depths of 318 feet (97 m).

FAMILY BOTHIDAE

115. CALIFORNIA HALIBUT — *Paralichthys californicus*

(California ←→ parallel fish)
Identification: In this family the eyes are usually but not always on the left side. The California halibut has an abrupt, high arch of the lateral line over the pectoral fin and a large mouth, the maxillary extends beyond the eye.
the maxillary extends beyond the eye.
Size: Length to 60 inches (152 cm). Weight to 72 lbs. (33 kg).
Range and Habitat: Quillayute River, Washington to Magdalena Bay, Baja California and an isolated population in the upper Gulf of California; on mud and sand bottoms; to depths of 300 feet (92 m).

B. Mulcahy

112. BLACKEYE GOBY

113. BLUEBANDED GOBY

C. Jones

C. Turner

114. ZEBRA GOBY

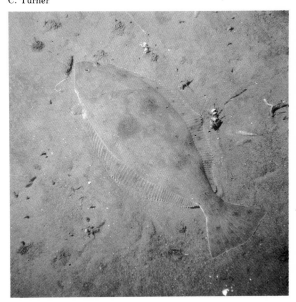

115. CALIFORNIA HALIBUT

116. FANTAIL SOLE
Xystreurys liolepis
(Smooth scale ←→ wide raker)

Identification: The fantail sole has large reddish-brown spots on the side, one under the tip of the long pectoral fin and one near the caudal peduncle. The pectoral fin is larger than the head as measured from the snout to the back edge of the gill cover.
Size: Length to 20 inches (51 cm).
Range and Habitat: Monterey Bay, California to Gulf of California; on sand and mud bottoms; in depths of 15 to 260 feet (5-79 m).

117. PACIFIC SANDDAB
Citharichthys sordidus
(Sordid ←→ rib fish)

Identification: There are four species of sanddabs along our coast and the three shallow water species can be separated by in-hand examination using the following: If the pectoral fin is bent forward, the tips reaches to about middle eye, it is the Pacific sanddab; if the tip of the pectoral fin does not reach the eye, it is the speckled sanddab, *C. stigmaeus* (not illustrated); if the first rays of the pectoral fin are longer than the head, it is the longfin sanddab, *C. xanthostigina* (not illustrated).
Size: *C. sordidus*, length to 16 inches; *C. stigmaeus*, to 6.7 inches; *C. xanthostigina*, to 10 inches (41, 17, 25 cm).
Range and Habitat: *C. sordidus*, Bering Sea to Cape San Lucas, Baja California; *C. stigmaeus*, Montague Island, Alaska to Magdalena Bay, Baja California; *C. xanthostigina*, Monterey Bay to Costa Rica; all on sand and mud bottoms; in depths of 30 to 1,800, 10 to 1,200 and 8 to 660 feet, respectively (9-553, 3-368 and 2-203 m).

FAMILY PLEURONECTIDAE

118. PACIFIC HALIBUT
Hippoglossus stenolepis
(Horse tongue; narrow scale)

Identification: Except for starry flounders members of this family have eyes on the right side. Pacific halibut have an elongated diamond shaped body and the eyes are always on the right side. In addition, the mouth is not as large as is the California halibut, the maxillary reaches only to the anterior edge of the eye.
Size: Length to 105 inches (267 cm). Weight to 800 lbs. (363 kg).
Range and Habitat: Sea of Japan and Bering Sea to Santa Rosa Island, California; on sand and mud bottoms; in depths of 20 to 360 feet (6-110 m).

119. ROCK SOLE
Lepidopsetta bilineata
(Two-lined ←→ scale flounder)

Identification: The rock sole has a dorsal branch of the lateral line that extends toward the tail and rough scales.
Size: Length to 23.5 inches (60 cm).
Range and Habitat: Sea of Japan and Bering Sea to Tanner Bank, California; on rocky and soft bottoms; in depths of 50 to 1200 feet (15-368 m).

116. FANTAIL SOLE

117. PACIFIC SANDDAB

R. Rosenthal

118. PACIFIC HALIBUT

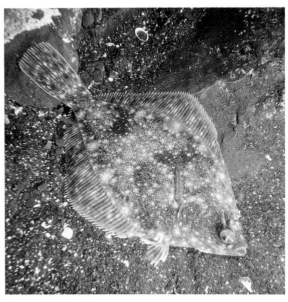

119. ROCK SOLE

120. SAND SOLE
Psettichthys melanostictus
(Flounder fish; black specks)

Identification: The sand sole has the first 4 or 5 dorsal rays that are elongated and free from the membrane that connects the fin rays.
Size: Length to 21 inches (53 cm).
Range and Habitat: Bering Sea to El Segundo, California; on sand and mud bottoms; in depths from 5 to about 600 feet (2-184 m).

121. ENGLISH SOLE
Parophrys vetulus
(Near eyebrow; old man)

Identification: The English sole has a pointed head and the lateral line lacks a high arch over the pectoral fin. The edge of one eye is visible from the blind side.
Size: Length to 22.5 inches (57 cm).
Range and Habitat: Northwest Alaska to San Cristobal Bay, Baja California; on sand and mud bottoms; from shallow bays to depths of 1,000 feet (307 m).

122. DIAMOND TURBOT
Hypsopsetta guttulata
(Deep flounder; with small spots)

Identification: The diamond shaped body with light blue spots and the white underside with lemon yellow coloring near the mouth and margin of the head are the best characters for identification.
Size: Length to 18 inches (46 cm).
Range and Habitat: Cape Mendocino, California to Magdalena Bay, Baja California and an isolated population in upper Gulf of California; on mud and sand bottoms; in depths of 5 to 150 feet (2-46 m).

123. CURLFIN TURBOT
Pleuronichthys decurrens
(Side fish; running down)

Identification: The best character to look for is the 9 or more anterior dorsal rays that extend onto the blind side; the first ray is located below a line drawn between the upper corner of the mouth and the base of the pectoral fin.
Size: Length to 14.5 inches (37 cm).
Range and Habitat: Northwest Alaska to Cedros Island, Baja California; on sand and mud bottoms; in depths of 60 to 1,146 feet (18-352 m).

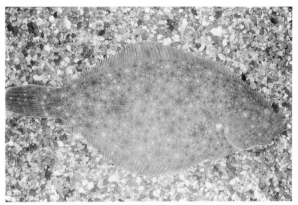

120. SAND SOLE

121. ENGLISH SOLE

122. DIAMOND TURBOT

123. CURLFIN TURBOT

124. C-O TURBOT

Pleuronichthys coenosus
(Muddy ←→ side fish)

Identification: C-O turbots have only 5 or 6 dorsal rays on the blind side, and 2 distinctive marks on the tail: the anterior mark in the form of a half-moon, the posterior mark in the form of a large dark blotch.

Size: Length to 14 inches (36 cm).

Range and Habitat: Southeastern Alaska to Cape Colnett, Baja California; on rocky and soft bottoms; in depths to 966 feet (296 m).

125. STARRY FLOUNDER

Platichthys stellatus
(Starry ←→ flat fish)

Identification: The eyes of the starry flounder can be either on the right or left side. They have dark bars on the dorsal and anal fins and very rough scales on the eyed side.

Size: Length to 36 inches (91 cm).

Range and Habitat: Sea of Japan and Arctic Alaska to Santa Barbara, California; on soft bottoms; in depths of 2 to 900 feet (1-275 m).

FAMILY MOLIDAE

126. COMMON MOLA

Mola mola
(Millstone; millstone)

Identification: The small mouth, lack of a distinct tail fin, shape of body and elongated dorsal and anal fins are very distinctive.

Natural History: Molas feed on jellyfish. They apparently are inshore along the California coast in late summer and fall to be cleaned of external parasites by cleaners such as senorita (98) and sharpnose surfperch (87).

Size: Estimated length to 157 inches (400 cm); estimated weight to 3,300 lbs. (1,500 kg).

Range and Habitat: Warm and temperate seas of the world; on our coast north to British Columbia; pelagic.

L. Laurent

124. C-O TURBOT

K. Lucas

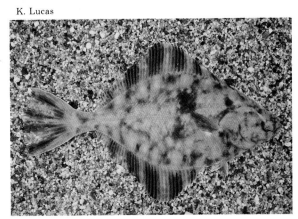

125. STARRY FLOUNDER

C. Turner

126. COMMON MOLA

BIBLIOGRAPHY

Baxter, John L. 1960. *Inshore Fishes of California.* 3rd Rev. Ed., California Department of Fish and Game, Sacramento. 80 pp.

Fitch, John E. 1969. *Offshore Fishes of California.* 4th Rev Ed., California Department of Fish and Game, Sacramento. 80 pp.

Fitch, John E. and Robert J. Lavenberg. 1968. *Deep-water Teleostean Fishes of California*, University of California Press, Berkeley. 155 pp.

_____. 1971. *Marine Food and Game Fishes of California*, University of California Press, Berkeley. 179 pp.

_____. 1975. *Tidepool and Nearshore Fishes of California*, University of California Press, Berkeley. 156 pp.

Gotshall, Daniel W. 1982. *Marine Animals of Baja California: A Guide to the Common Fish and Invertebrates.* Sea Challengers, Los Osos, Calif. 112 ppg.

Hart, J. L. 1973. *Pacific Fishes of Canada.* Fish Research Board of Canada, Bulletin (180): 740 pp.

Herald, Earl S. 1961. *Living Fishes of the World.* Doubleday and Co., New York. 301 pp.

_____. 1972. *Fishes of North America.* Doubleday and Co., New York, 254 pp.

Miller, Daniel J. and Robert N. Lea. 1976. *Guide to the Coastal Marine Fishes of California*, California Department of Fish and Game, Fish Bulletin (157). 249 pp.

Thompson, Donald A., Lloyd T. Findley, and Alex N. Kerstitch. 1979. *Reef Fishes of the Sea of Cortez.* John Wiley and Sons, New York. 302 pp.

INDEX TO COMMON NAMES

INDEX TO SCIENTIFIC NAMES

HABITATS OF COMMON FISHES
BY GEOGRAPHIC AREAS

SOUTHEASTERN ALASKA AND BRITISH COLUMBIA

Shallow Reefs and Kelp Beds
(3 - 15m)

Blackeye goby
Buffalo sculpin
Kelp greenling
Lingcod
Northern ronquil
Quillback rockfish
Rock greenling
Striped surfperch

Deep Reef (15 - 50m)
China rockfish
Copper rockfish
Yelloweye rockfish
Yellowtail rockfish

Sand and Mud Bottoms
Big skate
Dogfish
Pacific halibut
Pacific sanddab
Ratfish
Rock sole
Starry flounder

WASHINGTON AND OREGON

Shallow Reefs and Kelp Beds
Blackeye goby
Cabezon
Kelp greenling
Lingcod
Painted greenling
Pile surfperch
Rock greenling
Striped surfperch

Deep Reefs
Canary rockfish
China rockfish
Copper rockfish
Puget Sound rockfish
Wolf-eel
Yelloweye rockfish

Sand and Mud Bottoms
Dogfish
Pacific sanddab
Sand sole
Starry flounder

NORTHERN CALIFORNIA
(Crescent City to San Francisco)

Shallow Reefs and Kelp Beds
Black rockfish
Blackeye goby
Blue rockfish
Cabezon
Kelp greenling
Lingcod
Painted greenling
Pile surfperch
Rock greenling
Striped surfperch

Deep Reefs
China rockfish
Yelloweye rockfish
Yellowtail rockfish

Sand and Mud Bottoms
Pacific sanddab

CENTRAL CALIFORNIA
(San Francisco to Avila Beach)

Shallow Reefs and Kelp Beds
Black-and-yellow rockfish
Blackeye goby
Blue rockfish
Cabezon
Gopher rockfish
Kelp greenling
Kelp rockfish
Lingcod
Olive rockfish
Painted greenling
Pile surfperch
Striped surfperch

Deep Reefs
Copper rockfish
Rosy rockfish
Smooth ronquil
Vermilion rockfish

Sand and Mud Bottoms
Curlfin turbot
Pacific sanddab
Spotted cusk-eel

Pelagic
Blue shark
Common mola

SOUTHERN CALIFORNIA
(Avila Beach to San Diego)

Shallow Reefs and Kelp Beds
Black surfperch
Blacksmith
Bluebanded goby
Garibaldi

Halfmoon
Horn shark
Kelp bass
Kelp rockfish
Lavender sculpin
Opaleye
Senorita
Sheephead

Deep Reefs
Bocaccio
Calico rockfish
Flag rockfish
Honeycomb rockfish
Starry rockfish
Squarespot rockfish
Treefish
Vermilion rockfish

Sand and Mud Bottoms
Angel shark
Bat ray
California halibut
C-O turbot
Diamond turbot
Pacific sanddab

Pelagic
Blue shark
Jack mackerel
Common mola

NORTHERN BAJA CALIFORNIA

Shallow Reefs and Kelp Beds
Blacksmith
Garibaldi
Halfmoon
Kelp bass
Opaleye
Rock wrasse
Senorita
Sheephead

Deep Reefs
Ocean whitefish
Scythemarked butterflyfish
Starry rockfish

Sand and Mud Bottoms
Angel shark
Bat ray
California halibut
C-O turbot
Leopard shark

Pelagic
Blue shark
Jack mackerel
Common mola

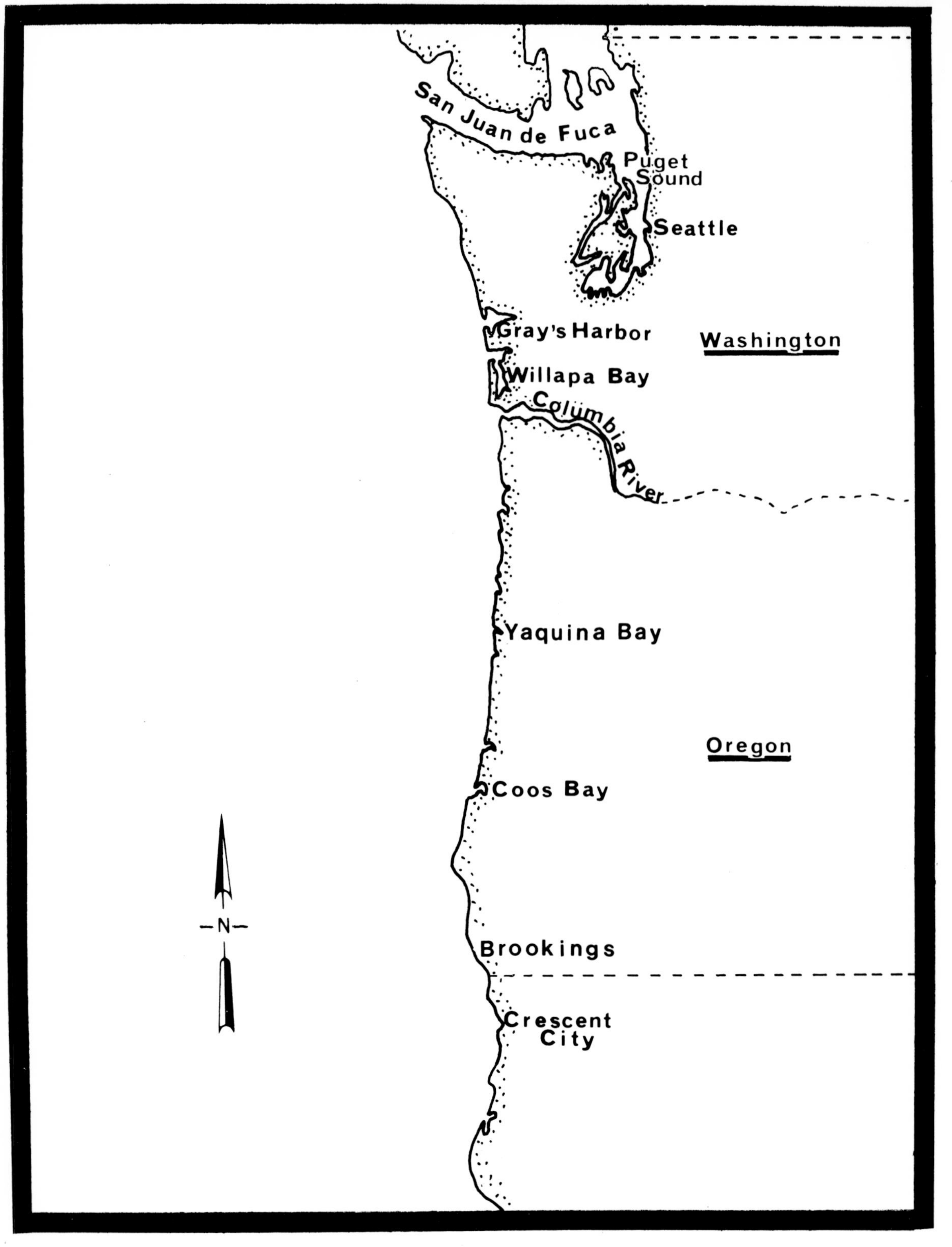

San Juan de Fuca

Puget Sound

Seattle

Gray's Harbor

Washington

Willapa Bay

Columbia River

Yaquina Bay

Oregon

Coos Bay

—N—

Brookings

Crescent City

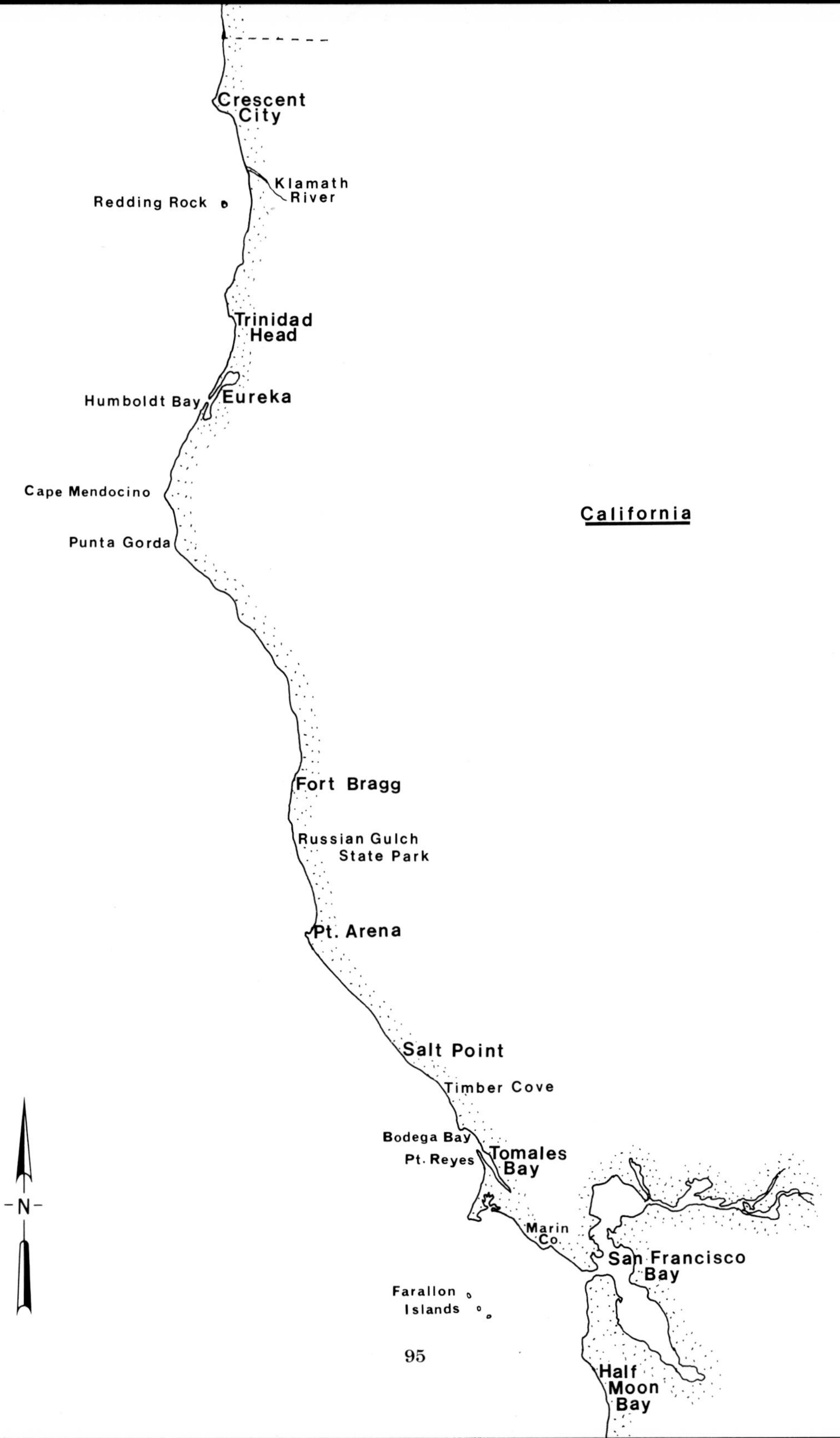

Crescent City

Klamath River

Redding Rock

Trinidad Head

Humboldt Bay
Eureka

Cape Mendocino

Punta Gorda

California

Fort Bragg

Russian Gulch State Park

Pt. Arena

Salt Point

Timber Cove

Bodega Bay
Pt. Reyes
Tomales Bay

Marin Co.

San Francisco Bay

Farallon Islands

Half Moon Bay

-N-

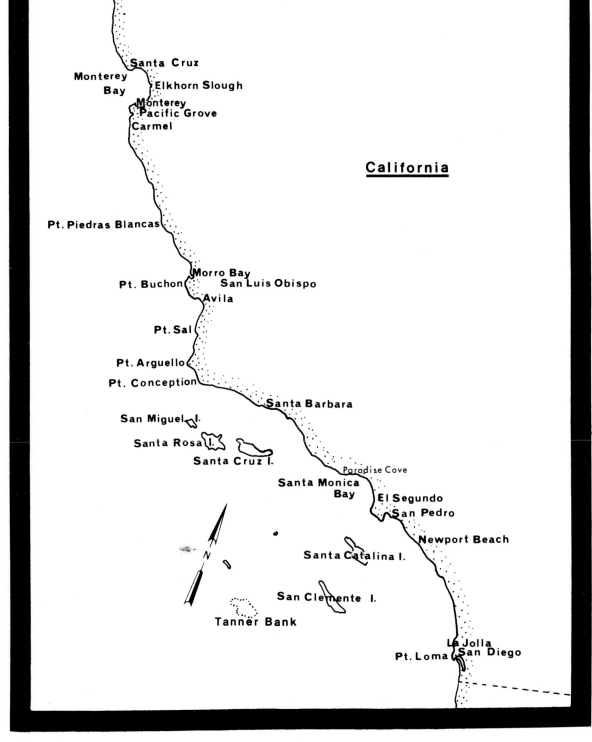

California

Santa Cruz
Monterey Bay
Elkhorn Slough
Monterey
Pacific Grove
Carmel

Pt. Piedras Blancas

Morro Bay
Pt. Buchon
San Luis Obispo
Avila
Pt. Sal
Pt. Arguello
Pt. Conception
Santa Barbara

San Miguel I.
Santa Rosa I.
Santa Cruz I.

Paradise Cove
Santa Monica Bay
El Segundo
San Pedro
Newport Beach

Santa Catalina I.

San Clemente I.
Tanner Bank

La Jolla
Pt. Loma
San Diego

N